STONES OF REMEMBRANCE

LIZ DUNSDON

WESTBOW
PRESS®
A DIVISION OF THOMAS NELSON
& ZONDERVAN

WestBow Press books may be ordered through booksellers or by contacting:

WestBow Press
A Division of Thomas Nelson & Zondervan
1663 Liberty Drive
Bloomington, IN 47403
www.westbowpress.com
1 (866) 928-1240

ISBN: 978-1-5127-8777-1 (sc)
ISBN: 978-1-5127-8776-4 (hc)
ISBN: 978-1-5127-8778-8 (e)

Library of Congress Control Number: 2017907637

Print information available on the last page.

WestBow Press rev. date: 5/19/2017

CONTENTS

CHAPTER 1

Introduction

The size of a challenge should never be measured by what we have to offer. It will never be enough. Furthermore, provision is God's responsibility, not ours. We are merely called to commit what we have—even if it's no more than a sack lunch.
—CHARLES R. SWINDOLL

On a recent holiday to St. Anthony, Newfoundland, I learned about the life of Dr. Wilfred Grenfell, who lived there in the late 1800s and early 1900s. He was an amazing man who affected the lives of the destitute fishermen living along the coast of Labrador and Newfoundland. Grenfell was a young doctor in England when he came to know Christ after hearing Dwight L. Moody speak. He felt God was calling him to join the Royal National Mission to Deep Sea Fishermen. He traveled to Newfoundland and Labrador to help provide medical and spiritual care to the fishermen and their families. He practiced medicine all along this barren coast.

Life was tough, to say the least, but Grenfell worked tirelessly to improve the quality of people's lives. He built hospitals, started schools and orphanages, wrote books, and helped set up a series of outpost nursing stations. He helped communities start gardens to fight the scurvy and beriberi he encountered among the coastal fisherman and their families. He helped the fishermen start their own fishery and cannery so they would receive better returns

1

on their work. He brought in artists to teach the women how to create beautiful rugs and clothing to sell to a larger market; he also used these artists as a way to tell them about God's love. He was a remarkable man. One story tells of how he set off in a blizzard in his kayak because medical help was needed in an outpost about ten kilometers away. His kayak sank, and he spent several days and nights floating on an ice floe before he was finally found. Grenfell influenced the lives of many people for their own good. His story is a testimony of what one person with God can accomplish. Amazing!

It is so easy to compare our lives with someone like Grenfell and come up short. I am amazed whenever I encounter or read about people like Grenfell, but I also feel a sense of my own inadequacies. God continues to remind me that I may feel like an ordinary person, but I am loved by an extraordinary God who dwells in me. God in me, living in and through me, is more important than my strengths, abilities, or limitations. I am slowly learning that my strength, peace, and limited wisdom come from the day-to-day consistency of entwining my life with Jesus. It is not how much a person accomplishes in this life as set out by the world's standards, but it is knowing God and fulfilling the purpose He created us for.

With this in mind, I finally sat down to write this book, which I have felt God urging me to do. My reason for writing is not to pour out my sad journey with cancer but to share how God loves to bless us in our brokenness and give us hope and new life in the midst of our struggles. I want to share how God works mightily on our behalf when we call out to Him. May God bless the words I have written. May they be an encouragement and a challenge to live your life in the hope that only comes from God. May you reflect on the blessings showered on you by the God who walks with you through the storm. Be thankful, and never stop believing that you are constantly loved by an extraordinary God who will never leave or forsake you. Let your heart be awed by His goodness. God may not fix your negative situations, but He promises to walk beside you to help you find a new hope and new life so you can carry on with living in confidence and purpose.

I hope this book will help and encourage you in whatever trials you are facing. There are so many people who face tremendous challenges, so I keep asking myself, *What could I possibly say that would help?* At times I was torn about whether to write this book, but as Jeremiah 20:9 (NIV) says, "But if I say, 'I will not mention his word or speak anymore in his name,' his word is in my heart like a fire, a fire shut up in my bones. I am weary of holding it in; indeed, I cannot." I want to shout out to the world that God is good. He is alive, and He sees me, knows all about me, and has wonderful plans for my life—just as He has for yours.

This is one of the verses given to me when I started to write: "Open wide your mouth and I will fill it" (Psalm 81:10b NIV). My constant prayer as I write is to ask God to fill my mouth with words that will encourage others to go beyond the scars and brokenness to see the beauty God wants to work in willing lives. He wants to work with you and me to create beauty in our lives in spite of the scars and ashes. His plans are to bring us a hope and a future if we are committed to allowing Him to work in and through us.

Luke tells the story of Jesus riding into Jerusalem shortly before He was crucified. The crowds clamored around Jesus in celebration. Luke 19:37–40 (NIV) says, "When he came near the place where the road goes down the Mount of Olives, the whole crowd of disciples began joyfully to praise God in loud voices for all the miracles they had seen: 'Blessed is the king who comes in the name of the Lord!' 'Peace in heaven and glory in the highest!' Some of the Pharisees in the crowd said to Jesus, 'Teacher, rebuke your disciples!' 'I tell you,' he replied, 'if they keep quiet, the stones will cry out.'" I like the picture of even the rocks crying out to tell of God's miracles and glory. If the rocks can speak, then I also need to share what God continues to do for me.

The Holy Spirit fills me with words that I cannot hold inside anymore. May you see what an extraordinary God can do in and

through a very ordinary woman and know that He wants to do this
and so much more in your life because He loves you.

Jesus looked at them and said, "With man this is
impossible, but with God all things are possible."
—Matthew 19:26

I love the LORD, for he heard my voice;
he heard my cry for mercy.
Because he turned his ear to me,
I will call on him as long as I live.
The cords of death entangled me,
the anguish of the grave came over me;
I was overcome by distress and sorrow.
Then I called on the name of the LORD:
"LORD, save me!"
The LORD is gracious and righteous;
our God is full of compassion.
The LORD protects the unwary;
when I was brought low, he saved me.
Return to your rest, my soul,
for the LORD has been good to you.
—Psalm 116:1–7 NIV

However, as it is written: "What no eye has seen, what no
ear has heard, and what no human mind has conceived"—
the things God has prepared for those who love him.
—2 Corinthians 2:9 NIV

CHAPTER 2

First Cancer

*The world has changed and it's going to keep changing, but
God never changes; so we are safe when we cling to Him.*
—CHARLES R. SWINDOLL

Cancer, like most struggles, has a quiet way of sneaking up on
you and catching you unaware. It is not something you can
prepare for ahead of time. If I see something coming down the road,
I like to get ready so I am not taken off guard. I did not see cancer
coming, and it initially knocked me flat on my face. I was not ready
to deal with cancer. I was a forty-eight-year-old wife and mother of
three teenage daughters who were pushing their boundaries to the
limit and beyond. I worked as a teacher, and I felt like I was running
a full-time taxi service for all our daughters' sporting and social
events. I was too busy for breast cancer. I did not have the time
or energy to deal with it. I had some very serious talks with God,
asking Him if He was aware of what was going on. It sounds quite
ridiculous now looking back on my attitude and thought processes,
but they were what they were.

I could not understand how God thought I could handle any
more. I would quote His word and ask for God to get rid of the
cancer; I would ask Him to let me get on with my all-consuming
life. Each time I prayed, I would hear the words from Psalm 46:10
(NIV): "He says, 'Be still, and know that I am God; I will be exalted

among the nations, I will be exalted."' I felt He was constantly telling me to be still and just trust Him. This was very difficult, since I felt so busy and pulled in all directions to do all that was expected of me—or at least to do all I expected of myself. I was just barely keeping my head above the water, and now cancer? The "be still" was exactly what I needed to learn, but it was not an easy or fast transition from marathon swimmer to just staying afloat by the grace of God. God slowly showed me how to slow down, stay focused on Him, rest in His presence, and let Him carry the load. I struggled to give control of my life and my loved ones into His hands and leave them there. I found it difficult to give God control over in my little corner of the world. I slowly learned and was amazed that everything could carry on just fine without me. Not easy. Jesus tells us in John 16:33 (NIV), "I have told you these things, so that in me you may have peace. In this world you will have trouble. But take heart! I have overcome the world." Why should I be surprised or expect my life to be easy or different from anyone else's life.

A few years before I encountered cancer, a lady in our church had gotten cancer, and I had watched her battle this disease. Actually, both she and her young daughter were both battling cancer at the same time. I finally concluded I could never handle something like this. I remember one day talking with God about cancer and telling Him (notice I was telling God!) that if I ever got cancer, life would be over because I would never take chemo. That was it. I guess I figured that dying was easier than having to give control over to God and stepping into the unknown in total trust. It never occurred to me that something good could come out of my fear and brokenness. God has continued to amaze me with His love as I have given cancer and all it entails to Him.

At the beginning, I was sure God would realize my extreme fear of chemo and would never allow me to be in position to have to face those fears. I have an abundance of food and drug allergies, so I decided that chemo would cause even worse reactions. I was soon to learn that God so often takes our greatest fears and shows us they are only the foolishness of man.

Our family had gone away for a tropical Christmas vacation. We had never done anything like this before and were so excited. The Norwalk virus ran through our resort, and I was sick one day. As I was lying in bed, I noticed a lump in my breast. I was upset but did not say anything because I did not want to ruin the holiday. I would check the lump multiple times each day in hopes that it had disappeared since the last time I felt it. I would try to convince myself that the lump was getting smaller and all would be just fine by the time we got home. It wasn't.

I visited my doctor upon returning from our holiday and started to learn about the process of hurry up and wait. I love to fix situations, but there was nothing I could do but wait. This was very frustrating and so against what I am comfortable with. I had to actually stop and give my fears to Jesus or go crazy as I carried on, pretending that all would be fine but fearing the worst. I still had not told anyone about my lump except my husband. My doctor sent me for various tests that took months and finally to a surgeon who operated and found that the lump was cancerous.

I had to slow down and "be still and know He is God." God was not surprised by what was happening in my life, though I was sure that for a time, He must have been sleeping or forgotten about me. I was the one who was surprised. I was going to have to face my fears and did not want to. I was going to have to change my lifestyle. It is strange how what seemed like such a mountain at the time looks so different from the other side now.

I had a lumpectomy and was supposed to start chemotherapy. You can imagine the battle going on in my mind. Remember I had told God that I would never take chemotherapy? I decided that I would go the "natural route" using a naturopath and leave the rest to God. Please do not think I am putting down naturopaths, because I do admire their work and use them. My dear friend who is a nurse confronted me and asked if I wanted to attend my daughters' graduations. She went on to say that if I intended to attend their graduations, then I better get my rear end down to the hospital and start chemo, except she said it in more direct terms! I felt like she had punched me in the stomach. Here I was so wrapped up in my own fears and trying to keep everyone from worrying about me that I was selfishly leaving everyone out. I hadn't thought about my family's input or what I was teaching our daughters about how to deal with the unexpected.

My mom's words came to mind. My mom had a serious talk with me over a cup of tea when our oldest daughter was a baby. It was a hard conversation, but she loved me enough to ask me the tough questions about what my lifestyle what was saying about my values, faith, and what I held dear. She reminded me that the way I actually lived my life would be more important than my words to my children. She went on to remind me that I would have the privilege of telling our children about how much Jesus loved each of them, but all would mean nothing if my life did not match up with my words. It hurt to be confronted about my lax lifestyle, but my mom's words did change my life. As parents, I am sure you know you can relate to have felt the responsibility of little eyes constantly watching. God patiently showed me how to change as I allowed Him to work in my heart and life.

Now here I stood facing cancer, cowering in fear. What was I showing my daughters and husband? I had often encouraged my daughters with 2 Timothy 1:7 (NKJV), "For God hath not given us the spirit of fear; but of power, and of love, and of a sound mind." The fear I felt did not come from God, so I started to claim the power, love, and a sound mind of this promise. Once I got over focusing on the need to run, I could hear the promises and peace God had wanted to give me all along. I began to stand up to the fear with the help of Jesus, claiming the promise in Philippians 4:13 (NLT), "I can do all things through Christ who strengthens me."

God had to speak loudly to me for a while before I finally realized He was in control, this disease was no surprise to Him, and

He would be going with me through the chemo. I had to get beyond my fear and realize I needed these drugs so I could stay alive and be with the people I love. I committed to asking God daily to show me how to think positive. I started to be thankful for the drugs I would be taking. I would give thanks for all the nurses, doctors, and researchers who were given the wisdom to make these drugs and the people who would help me through. My attitude started to change when I became thankful. My friend Lily has a stock answer to life's problems. She says, "Just get over it!" It was time for me to stop whining, get over it, and get on with whatever lay ahead.

Our Lord is so patient and loving. He meets us right where we are. He knows our greatest fears and needs. He sends His word to encourage and strengthen our souls. I found reassurance in Isaiah 43:1b–4 (NIV), where God was showing the nation of Israel His love and care for them in their trial.

> Do not fear, for I have redeemed you; I have summoned you by name; you are mine. When you pass through the waters, I will be with you; and when you pass through the rivers, they will not sweep over you. When you walk through the fire, you will not be burned; the flames will not set you ablaze. For I am the LORD your God, the Holy One of Israel, your Savior; I give Egypt for your ransom, Cush and Seba in your stead. Since you are precious and honored in my sight, and because I love you, I will give people in exchange for you, nations in exchange for your life.

Cancer made me transfer what I knew in my head and heart about God's grace into actions. I believed God always was with me and protected me, but I now had to step out and act on my faith. It was not enough to ask God to heal me and just sit there crying. I needed to learn to rely on God to get me through chemo

9

if I wanted to get better. My children needed to see how I lived out the promises I profess to believe—promises such as, "I can do all things through Christ who strengthens me" (Philippians 4:13 NIV). His grace is always sufficient. God proved this to be true each and every day. My teenagers were going through quite the rebellious period at this time, and in so many ways the cancer was just a secondary issue. God walked with me and gave me the strength and wisdom to deal with not only cancer but also rebellious teens. Our God is so much bigger than cancer and rebellious teens. Circumstances may feel like we are being swamped or incinerated, but we are still safe in the hands of our Lord. Romans 8:37–39 (NIV) says, "No, in all these things we are more than conquerors through him who loved us. For I am convinced that neither death nor life, neither angels nor demons, neither the present nor the future, nor any powers, neither height nor depth, nor anything else in all creation, will be able to separate us from the love of God that is in Christ Jesus our Lord."

When it came time to start chemo, I felt so protected in the love of God. I was still afraid, but I was not terrified. I knew God would never leave me nor forsake me. I loved the Psalm where David calls out to the Lord and paints a picture of being protected under a wing as a mother hen protects her chicks. Psalm 57:1 (NIV) says, "Have mercy on me, my God, have mercy on me, for in you I take refuge. I will take refuge in the shadow of your wings until the disaster has passed." I could see myself held close to God under His wings each time I got drugs or was sick afterward. I made it through the treatments. The promise from Philippians, "I can do all things through Christ who gives me strength" began to take on a whole new meaning. I realized that "all things" also included all the things we can't do on our own. Stepping out in faith, trusting the Lord would walk with me into the future, whatever it held, taught me that Christ in us is our strength. We begin to see and understand how Christ works in and through us when we reach the end of our limits and have to venture on. The glory is given to God and not to us. We do not carry on because we have the human strength, but Christ gives us strength each day to face the challenges we will come against.

My first detour with cancer continued until the day I turned fifty. I had been taking further treatment with Herceptin, which hopefully would stop the likelihood of cancer returning. This drug had just been approved to be used as a preventative treatment. What looked like such a promising drug was not for me as it caused damage to the muscles that pump blood in my heart. I had to stop the drug early in the regime after only a few treatments. I only tell you about Herceptin because God was not finished using this drug and was going to do something awesome with it in the future. I will tell you more later!

Most of my fears proved foolish, and I sailed through my rounds of treatment. I quickly lost my long hair, which was hard, but I learned a new technique of hair removal. My hair was falling out rapidly, and you could find clumps of hair all over. It was gross. I was vacuuming the falling hair one morning when I came upon a terrific idea. Why not vacuum my hair out? I could use the hose, and swish, the hair would be gone. I got everyone up and let everyone try to make crop circles, runways, or designs until I was totally bald. It was fun and made us laugh. We no longer had to contend with hair clumps or fretting over the hair falling out. I have since done this method twice more. It is always a highlight for my husband! The first time I went bald, I felt self-conscious and would always wear a wig or hat if I was out of the house. I did not even get a picture of myself being bald. Since then I have gotten used to being bald, and it no longer bothers me if people stare or make comments. Baldness is just part of life.

The treatments made me very tired but not really sick. I would puke a bit, but as I have learned, I am good at puking! I can hug the toilet bowl a few times, and then I feel great. Strange, but true. I would get a migraine headache exactly a week after a treatment that would last the day. Guess what! Migraines have always made me puke, so at least I was consistent. I was emotionally drained but physically better than I thought I would be.

I originally thought of cancer as just another disaster in my life. Not anymore. I have learned how to allow God to work through the cancer to bring me to a place where I could slowly let go of my fears, my plans, and my loved ones and just trust that He was at work even if I did not understand. Up to this point, I had prayed mightily for my children, given them to God, and then walked beside God trying to fix things up and hurry up His timing. Some people may have their eyes opened to their pride and lack of trust in God through an easier process, but I seem to do things the hard way. God slowly pried my hands open and helped me release my cares and worries to Him.

Through this time of my first encounter with cancer, it grew increasingly easier to give my daughters to God and to trust them into His care. Life had not gotten easier, but God had gotten bigger. One night I remember being so sick and tiptoeing downstairs to pray after everyone was asleep. I went off by myself so I could pour my heart out to God openly without worrying about disturbing my sleeping family. I was quite ill and was heartsick, wondering if I died who would be there for my family. A mother's love and guidance is different than a father's—not necessarily better or worse, but different. I agonized over who would pray for them if I was gone. I lay curled up on the bed, sobbing before the Lord. He didn't chastise me for my lack of faith, but I could feel His arms wrapped around me. I heard Him speak in my heart, and He said, "Liz, I have loved you with an everlasting love." Then He showed me a picture of how he held my daughters close in the palm of His hand and reminded me of a verse and promise He had given me earlier for each of them.

My heart was overwhelmed with His love and care. He heard and understood a mother's love for her children. He had already prepared verses and given them to me ahead of time so I would have them when I needed to pray for my children. Whether I was there or not, God was watching over our daughters, had plans for them, and would never quit calling them. How I praised God that night for meeting me, for what He was doing and what He was going to do in the future. He was and still is in control. It was about learning to trust and obey as I waited for God's timing.

A huge burden was lifted from my shoulders after this meeting with God. I felt a calm or peace in my soul whenever fears or disasters flared up to do with cancer or teenage choices. I am still human and still tried to take things back from God at times and ran around like Miss Fix-It, but over time, it has become easier to give circumstances back to God and leave them with Him. God fixes broken lives and hearts way in ways we can't understand. We have to trust Jesus enough to allow Him to work. Jesus is a gentleman and will not walk all over us and push His way in. He desires only the best for us, but we have to be willing to let Him work. I began to understand the verses in Jeremiah 29:11–14a (NIV), "'For I know the plans I have for you,' declares the LORD, 'plans to prosper you and not to harm you, plans to give you hope and a future. Then you will call on me and come and pray to me, and I will listen to you. You will seek me and find me when you seek me with all your heart. I will be found by you,' declares the LORD, 'and will bring you back from captivity.'" This promise was given to Israel seventy years before they would be released from captivity in Babylon. God works on His timing, not ours, but His promises are true.

I read or heard somewhere that when we hold our fears, sins, hurts, injustices, anger, or whatever close, we do not leave room for Jesus to heal. It is like holding our problems in a tightly fisted hand. Your fist is full of darkness. Your fist only holds your problem and darkness. Open your fist up to Jesus, and let His light and love wipe away the darkness. Let go of the lies you believe and give them to Jesus. You will be amazed with what He can do with your life. It will be something far better than you ever hoped or even dreamed of.

I will end this chapter with this promise from Proverbs 3:5–6 (NIV): "Trust in the LORD with all your heart and lean not on your own understanding; in all your ways submit to him, and he will make your paths straight." I don't know about you, but I want to walk the paths that the Lord has set out for me. I usually end up floundering, stumbling, and falling on my face when I follow my own ways. You may not understand the path set before you to walk. It may not be of your choosing, but if this is where God leads you, then follow because that is where Jesus will be, and He promises to walk each step with you. Trust Jesus, and let Him awe you.

I lift up my eyes to the mountains—
where does my help come from?
My help comes from the Lord,
the Maker of heaven and earth.
He will not let your foot slip—
he who watches over you will not slumber;
indeed, he who watches over Israel
will neither slumber nor sleep.
The Lord watches over you—
the Lord is your shade at your right hand;
the sun will not harm you by day,
nor the moon by night.
The Lord will keep you from all harm—
he will watch over your life;
the Lord will watch over your coming and going
both now and forevermore.
—Psalm 121 (NIV)

When I am afraid, I will trust in you.
In God, whose word I praise,
in God I trust; I will not be afraid.
—Psalm 56:3–4 (NIV)

I remain confident of this:
I will see the goodness of the Lord

in the land of the living.
Wait for the Lord;
be strong and take heart
and wait for the Lord.
—Psalm 27:13–14 (NIV)

CHAPTER 3

Waiting

A teardrop on earth summons the King of heaven.
—CHARLES R. SWINDOLL

Cancer involves lots of hurry up and wait! There is the waiting for tests and then waiting for the doctors while you are hoping and praying with everything in you that the results will be positive. There are tests followed by more tests. The list seems endless. There is blood work, needle biopsies, x-rays, various scans, and biopsies before the results are known. There are surgeries to see if the tumor is cancerous and more or to remove the cancer, then the insertion of ports to use during chemo if needed. There are meeting with the oncologists to determine how to treat the cancer. There are so many tests and decisions to be made. Finally there is the waiting to see if the treatments are working. It can feel overwhelming at times.

The return of cancer is always there as a possibility that loves to get your mind going. Worrying does not help or change a thing. Matthew 6:27 (NIV) says, "Can any one of you by worrying add a single hour to your life?" We can see worrying is a waste of precious time and energy. When I looked past the worrying, I realized I was grieving as much as worrying. My life was different now, and I could not go back and have a "do over." What I used to consider as normal is different now. Does that make sense? It is okay to grieve for what you have lost, but do not stop there. Keep walking through the treatments with Jesus as He has wonderful treasures along the way.

My first episode of breast cancer involved continual waiting. The second time was no different. The continual process of opening my tight little fists and handing over the control to God never ends. I often wish life came with a remote control to fast forward through the wait times. I could not hurry up the test results. I could not hurry up the process. I could not take away the cancer by myself. I could not change what had invaded my life and body. I felt like I was just along for the ride, and I hated the feeling. I could not change what was happening, but God kept whispering to me day and night to be still and trust as he was in control. In Psalm 46:5, 10 (NIV), He says," God is within her, she will not fall; God will help her at break of day. ... Be still, and know that I am God; I will be exalted among the nations, I will be exalted in the earth." As I said before, this verse kept running through my head when anxiety came knocking on my door. I would stop and tell myself, "God is in control of everything. He knows what is going on, and He hears my prayers and is working on my behalf. Just stop and give these useless thoughts to God." All the worrying in the world will not change anything. I find the verse, "The Lord will fight for you; you need only to be still" in Exodus 14:14 (NIV) to be encouraging.

Max Lucado in *Life Lessons on Philippians* explains how the apostle Paul was able to remain positive in all circumstances. Let's be honest. Control is an illusion. We can't engineer problem-free events, and we can't make people live the way we want them to live. About the only thing we can control is our own response to life situations. Will we look for God in the midst of trouble? Will we trust that He is at work? Will we keep doing right no matter what? Will we choose to remain positive? Paul is a great role model for us. He absolutely refused to pursue his own agenda, because he saw himself as a mere servant of Christ. He made plans, but he held them in an open hand. When hard times came, his response wasn't to pout. It was to yield to God's authority by humbly saying, "Thy will be done."

Paul wrote these wonderful, encouraging words to the church in Philippi while he was in chains for telling others of Jesus. Philippians 4:6–7 (NIV) reads, "Do not be anxious about anything, but in every situation, by prayer and petition, with thanksgiving, present your requests to God. And the peace of God, which transcends all understanding, will guard your hearts and your minds in Christ Jesus."

I found myself drawing closer to God and the driving need to know or fix everything right *now* slowly gave way to peace. The time of waiting became a beautiful time of drawing closer to God, being still, and letting go. Psalm 55:10 (NIV) says, "Cast your cares on the LORD and he will sustain you; he will never let the righteous be shaken." He took my cares, and I claimed His promises that He was God and He would not allow me to be shaken.

God reminded me that there is usually a purpose to the waiting. It is a way of preparing us for the challenges that we will soon be facing. I would continue to learn the balance between cancer and rebellious teenagers and entrusting both into His hands. This was hard struggle. Cancer and treatments were hardly on my radar as I was too busy fighting for my children and family.

I had to leave home for seven weeks for radiation. The closest cancer clinic for radiation was in Kelowna, British Columbia, a nearly eight-hour drive away. I found the radiation treatments to be excruciatingly slow. It was so hard for me to leave our daughters, who were angry, hurting, and worried. My poor husband! It felt like my heart was ripping apart. Most nights one of our daughters would phone to vent and cry her heart out. It was painful being so far away. During my time away, I began to release my daughters to God and His care. I didn't have much a choice as I was so far away. They were at the age when they were trying to figure it out for themselves. I would sit for hours quilting if I had the energy. Other days I sat reading my Bible and praying for our daughters and giving them into God's hand. He would meet me each day and give me the strength to hold on.

One good thing that came out of me being away at radiation was that our daughters began to appreciate my cooking. Just before I left for radiation, my husband had brought home a box of tomatoes. I got busy one day and made seventeen pints of salsa. I guess it was delicious, though I never tasted any of it. My family had eaten it all during the time I was away! No one wanted to cook much, so I guess they lived on tomato soup and nachos. Dave threw in a few scrambled eggs and pork and beans. I was actually appreciated when I got home! At times teenagers find it hard to appreciate parents, so I soaked up the warmth. Thinking about all that salsa still makes me laugh.

God showed me that my daughters belonged to Him and He would call them back to Himself in His own way and in His own time. They needed to decide for themselves who they were and what they wanted to believe. They have all come back to the Lord with their own strong faith. God worked in their lives in amazing ways. The lesson God taught me through the hours and hours I spent on my knees praying for their safety was to trust. God was bigger than anything they got involved in. God was faithful. God used my daughters and cancer for a purpose. Part of waiting was to learn to trust even when I could not see how or where God was working. When you are in a difficult situation, ask God what He wants to teach you or others involved in your circumstances.

God hears each and every one of our prayers and answers them in His own way and on His own timetable. God says He has plans to prosper us and give us a hope and a future. We can't always understand why and how God answers, but they are always for our good. I can only see the cancer from my limited vision and focusing only on my desires. God sees the whole picture. He loves us, comforts us, and strengthens us for our fight or journey. It is so important to remember that God does not leave us to fight by ourselves but goes on this journey with each of us. Romans

18:24–25 (NIV) says, "For in this hope we were saved. But hope that is seen is no hope at all. Who hopes for what they already have? But if we hope for what we do not yet have, we wait for it patiently."

It is during the waiting time that our minds love to go to places that can rob us of our hope. At first I would allow my mind to go around in circles, trying to find an escape. Most of us always circle the worst-case scenarios! It was a feeling similar to being on a merry-go-round. My thoughts would continually circle around the negative and try to figure out way to get off the merry-go-round and make everything happy again.

The stories and information on the Internet would pound in the hopelessness. I quit reading the Internet and decided to ask God to send me wise health professionals to explain and guide me through decisions to be made. The discussions with the cancer doctors or chemo nurses were endlessly helpful—way better than the Internet. The sound advice given by these caregivers was clear, knowledgeable, and backed up by experience. God gave me peace about the decisions we decided upon. I would pray before each meeting and ask God to be in the room, to give wisdom and clarity of thought to both the doctors and myself.

I felt an ever-increasing desire to read the Bible. Each day I would pore over God's promises and find comfort in knowing how God hears, rescues, and walks with us just as He did when they were penned. His promises were faithful then, and they continue today. I loved Psalm 80:3 (NIV), which says, "Restore us, O God; make your face shine on us, that we may be saved." I would pray this verse when going through tests and feel the warmth of His face shining on me. I wasn't alone. He was with me, and His face was shining on me. The Psalms were mostly written by King David, who was a musician. The book of Psalms contains poems or songs that portray every human emotion there is. The Psalms became my prayers and strength when I felt overwhelmed during test procedures. I would focus on God's word and His promises rather than on the poking, prodding, and diagnoses.

Each time my results have come back as cancer. I found peace instead of fear or hopelessness. There were definitely times when I felt despair, but when I focused on Jesus and drew in close, the peace returned. Praise God for the wait time. Pastor Paul at the church I attend often refers to "waiting" in Isaiah 40:31 (KJV): "But they that wait upon the LORD shall renew their strength; they shall mount up with wings as eagles; they shall run, and not be weary; and they shall walk, and not faint." He explains that the original Hebrew word translated *wait* comes from a word meaning to twine together like in splicing a rope. Waiting on the Lord is twining our lives together with God. We twine our lives together with God by spending time with Him, in His word in worship and in prayer. One strand of rope may break, but when the strands are twined together, there is strength and durability. The twining with God makes us strong so we can mount up with wings as eagles. When we mount up on wings as eagles, we soar above. We can look down on our lives and troubles from a different view—God's view. To be able to do this, we must first spend the time in the Bible and in communion with the Lord to be closely entwine with Jesus. Then we can soar above with Jesus.

I urge you to wait upon the Lord, to twine your life with His. There will be many ups and downs ahead, but when your eyes are fixed on Jesus and walking with Him, then He will give you the strength, wisdom, and endurance to fight the battles ahead. Take your waiting time, and use it wisely to twine your life with God. Ask God to show you what He is doing in your life. Ask God to be given the ability to see events from His view. It will change your attitude.

The wait time was hard, but it was also a blessing. I had time to organize my personal life for what lay ahead. The wait time gave me time to twine my life with God so that not only would I have strength to meet the obstacles but to soar above them as an eagle does. I was reading about eagles and seagulls during storms. They spread their wings and soar high above the storm. The stronger the storm, the higher they fly. Believe me that I did not always soar.

There were many times when I could not leave the nest, but each time I stepped out in faith made it easier to soar the next time.

If you are going through a time of waiting and fearing the future, twine your life with God. Become so close to God that He fills every fiber of your being. Bind His word in your heart. When you pray, ask God not to just change your circumstances but to also change you and help you to grow toward Him. Be thankful for His presence and continued care right where you are, waiting. Then mount up on wings as eagles and soar with Jesus over the storm.

I think of the story of Joseph in the Bible. His life is one of waiting and struggles. God had a purpose and brought all the pieces together at just the right time for Joseph to be the man needed to save Egypt and his family from starvation. Joseph was given a dream that someday people would bow down before him. He told his brothers his dream, which angered them. His brothers already hated Joseph and were jealous that their father loved Joseph more than them. The brothers sold Joseph into slavery when he was still a teenager. Genesis 37:28 (NIV) says, "So when the Midianite merchants came by, his brothers pulled Joseph up out of the cistern and sold him for twenty shekels of silver to the Ishmaelites, who took him to Egypt." Joseph was sold and ended up in Egypt in the house of Potiphar. Joseph worked hard and was given the responsibility of overseeing his whole household. Potiphar's wife eventually became interested in Joseph and became angry when he kept rebuffing her. She eventually accused him of trying to rape her, and Joseph was thrown into prison.

Again Joseph worked diligently and was given the task of running the prison. Years passed. The pharaoh had a dream that no one could explain to him. His cupbearer remembered the time when he was in prison and Joseph had interpreted a dream for him and told Pharaoh about Joseph. God gave Joseph the ability to understand Pharaoh's dream. Egypt was going to have seven years of bountiful crops followed by seven years of severe drought, when nothing would grow. Joseph was given the job of preparing all of Egypt for the drought. He was second in command, only under Pharaoh, for all of Egypt.

Joseph was faithful in all he was given to do—even in trying circumstances. Eventually his brothers came to Egypt to get grain during the famine. They bowed down before Joseph as he was in charge of all the grain distribution, but they did not recognize him. People from all of Egypt and the surrounding areas would bow down before Joseph to ask for food that fulfilled the dream given to him when he was young. His brothers were terrified when they finally realized who Joseph was. Joseph forgave his brothers and brought his family to Egypt to survive as the famine would only get worse. God had a purpose for Joseph's life, but it took many years to come to fruition. He continued to grow and develop into the man who would be able to save Egypt and surrounding countries from starvation. Joseph continued to follow after God in spite of the many injustices dealt to him. Later he was able to explain his purpose to his brothers. Genesis 50:20 (NIV) says, "You intended to harm me, but God intended it for good to accomplish what is now being done, the saving of many lives." Look around at the events around you, and ask God what He wants you to learn as you wait.

When I am afraid, I will trust in you.
In God, whose word I praise, in God I trust;
I will not be afraid.
— Psalm 56:3–4 (NIV)

Take delight in the Lord,
and he will give you the desires of your heart.
Commit your way to the Lord;
trust in him and he will do this:
He will make your righteous reward shine like the dawn,
your vindication like the noonday sun.
Be still before the Lord
and wait patiently for him.
— Psalm 37:4–7 (NIV)

Whatever you have learned or received or heard
from me, or seen in me—put it into practice.
And the God of peace will be with you.
— Philippians 4:9 (NIV)

I have not stopped giving thanks for you, remembering
you in my prayers. I keep asking that the God of our Lord
Jesus Christ, the glorious Father, may give you the Spirit of
wisdom and revelation, so that you may know him better.
I pray that the eyes of your heart may be enlightened in
order that you may know the hope to which he has called
you, the riches of his glorious inheritance in his holy people,
and his incomparably great power for us who believe.
— Ephesians 1:16–19 (NIV)

As soon as I pray, you answer me; you
encourage me by giving me strength.
— Psalm 138:3 (NLT)

CHAPTER 4

Unstoppable People

We are all faced with a series of great opportunities
brilliantly disguised as impossible situations.
—CHARLES R. SWINDOLL

I love telling stories. Stories are inspiring, and they help me to get a glimpse of the essence of people. My favorites are about ordinary people who are not be deterred or defined by circumstances. The ones I remember and love telling about are the ones who faced great adversity but never gave up. They set out to accomplish something even when others told them it was impossible. I am a retired school teacher and used to love to share stories of adventure and overcoming obstacles with my class. Some of my favorite stories are about people who helped build our country into such a great nation.

One such story is of David Thompson. One winter while laid up with a broken leg, he read books to teach himself to be a surveyor. He went on to work for both the Hudson Bay Company and the Northwest Company, mapping the rivers of western Canada to set up fur-trading posts. He also surveyed and mapped much of the border between Canada and the United States. He traveled by canoe with his Métis wife and five of his youngest children mapping the rivers and landmarks of the western half of Canada. His leg never healed correctly after it was broken, so he struggled with a bad limp. He also was blind in one eye. He completed the daunting task of mapping the waterways to the Pacific Ocean with physical issues and a large family, but he had a purpose and would not turn back or let his disabilities stop him. His maps were so accurate that mapmakers later used his work as a standard.

I love to tell the story of my parents who packed up and immigrated to Canada when I was eleven. Our family left loved ones and friends for a dream of a better life but with a certainty that God was calling them to a new country. My parents had read the book *Grass Beyond the Mountains* by Rich Hobson and had decided to drive to north central British Columbia and explore. They fell in love with the country, which was filled with potential farmland, lakes, and rivers. Mom and Dad bought a farm in the bush outside of Fort Fraser, where we moved to the following year. My dad and grandpa had built a small two-room house the fall before we moved. There was nothing there on the farm but trees and a dream that something better was ahead. The road to our home was a clay track with grass growing up the middle. We spent a lot of time getting stuck or pushing vehicles up the muddy hills. There was no electricity or running water unless one of us kids ran up the hill carrying the buckets of water! We worked so hard in the beginning adjusting and turning the forest into a viable farm. My parents did not look at the enormous amount of work but saw beyond to what the farm would become someday. Those years growing up on the farm are such happy memories. I learned the value of hard work and trusting in God when things seemed impossible. We had very little materially, but my brothers and I grew up loved and constantly encouraged that we could accomplish whatever we set our minds to do. Mom and Dad shared their strong faith in God through their actions and words. I have been blessed with such a wonderful heritage.

Robyn, a friend and colleague, inspires me with how she has never given up. She went through cancer many years ago. Since, she has lost her husband in a tragic accident and her son to cancer. She is an amazing woman and a fighter. When she was initially told that she had stage 3 cancer, she told me that she looked into the mirror and said to herself, "You have a choice. You are in the biggest fight of your life right now. You can choose to give up, or you can choose to fight." She continued to look at her reflection and stated, "You are going to fight with every fiber of your being to beat this awful disease." Robyn decided that she had no choice but to fight. She was a mom, and her teenagers needed her. She owed it to them to fight because they needed a mom. She has fought and beat cancer and has continued fighting through her other heartbreaking losses. Robyn is an inspiration to me and many others.

Like these stories, the Bible is full of ordinary people who faced mighty challenges, adversity, or brokenness. Some failed, but many more were able to overcome obstacles or trials and carry on. Most people are changed as they struggle with tragedy or face disease, but even though they are changed, they carried on with life. I have wondered and prayed a lot about why some people can go on and live a productive life, but others become desolate and give up. I am continually impressed by the commitment and determination of ordinary people in the face of hardship. They may be daunted, but they fight on. The thought of caving in and giving up never occurs to them. These people have inspired me to never give up each time my cancer has returned.

For the last twelve years I have battled against a cancer that keeps coming back. I was originally diagnosed with stage 3 breast cancer. Almost seven years later, it returned to spread to my bones and lymph system. Cancer returned again last summer, with cancerous tumors throughout my brain. I say I have battled cancer because I have fought this disease with everything in me for myself and for my family. I refuse to give into this disease or let it define who I am. I am sure many people can relate to this feeling of constantly having to fight just to be. Many times I have fallen on my face and just whined and sniveled. I excel at this sometimes. Whining may last for a time, but I get back up, and with the help of God and loved ones, get on with the fight. I refuse to just roll over and die. My loved ones deserve nothing less than my very best.

I have chosen to put my hope and trust in Jesus who has given me the love, strength, and courage to battle when I became too weak on my own. I choose to put my trust in Jesus because He has continually proved Himself to be faithful. I've been told by some that my faith is just a crutch. We all have the right to decide what we believe. What you or others decide to believe about God does not change who God is, His never-ending love for everyone, or how He continues to share in my life daily. It would be like me denying the existence of the wind because I can't see it. I pray that this book encourages you to never give up regardless of where you put your hope.

Many people in their lives will face daunting challenges, tragedy, and hurts that rip their hearts apart. We live in a broken world and should not be surprised by these circumstances. Unfortunately, it is part of the human condition. These trials will dent us, bend us, and leave us with scars, but they will not destroy us unless we allow them to. While writing this book, I listened to countless stories of human pain. There is so much in life that is beyond our control. What we can control is our attitude, our determination, and our choices. These three attributes often determine how we live.

Throughout my illness, I have thought about how our bodies, spirits, and souls are central to our well-being. We need to care for our bodies so they do not give out on us when we need to be strong to fight. I have worked on being healthier ever since I became sick. I wish I had taken better care of my body along the way, but I cannot change that. I go for long walks every day. My husband and I love to kayak or go rock picking to get out in the fresh air. I have watched what I eat so my diet is balanced. I make a point of keeping busy. I taught school until I was unable to because I had no immunity. I clean house, cook, garden, and continue with the activities I did before becoming sick. I may have to do them slower, but I need to be busy and have a routine. The point is to keep my body strong and active.

Our souls are important in keeping a positive outlook. We

need to fill our lives with positive people who fill us up. These people are like a fresh breath of air. They revive and invigorate us. They will urge us on and keep us accountable. There are so many professionals available to help deal with tragedy. Reach out and find them. Talk to friends, family, and professionals to keep a healthy, active mind. I have found that God is my friend and confidant to depend upon. He has picked me up so many times and helped me get on to becoming the person He created me to be and to live the life He set out for me. He continually shows me that He only wants the best for me. That does not mean life will be easy or that I am not responsible for my part, but it means that the Lord will never leave me and will always go with me. The part I am responsible for are my thoughts and attitude. I can choose to dwell on the positive or the negative, which only sends me on a downward spiral.

Part of the following quote by Charles Swindoll is from the poem Attitude and one of my favorites. Years ago I put this on a poster at my desk at work and on my fridge at home as a constant reminder of my attitude and how it affects my life. If you take the time to really think about this quote, you will see it is very true.

> The longer I live, the more I realize the impact of attitude on life. Attitude, to me, is more important than facts. It is more important than the past, than education, than money, than circumstances, than failures, than successes, than what other people think or say or do. It is more important than appearance, giftedness or skill. It will make or break a company ... a church ... a home. The remarkable thing is we have a choice every day regarding the attitude we will embrace for that day. We cannot change our past ... we cannot change the fact that people will act in a certain way ... I am convinced that life is 10% what happens to me and 90% how I react to it. And so it is with you.

Spiritual well-being is a personal choice we each make. As I have said, I choose to chase after God because He has proved Himself worthy of my trust and praise. He fills my heart and spirit each and every day. We each have to decide where we are going to park our trust and faith. You may decide to put your faith in yourself, your job, your partner, or whatever, but we need something to trust and to fill up our inner beings. The love of my family and friends also fills me up inside with boundless love. I have so much to be thankful for.

Psalm 62:5 (NIV) says, "Find rest, O my soul, in God alone; my hope comes from him. He alone is my rock and my salvation; he is my fortress, I will not be shaken." The word *hope* in the original Hebrew refers to a cord or an attachment. Hope is like a cord running between God and myself. I choose to attach my cord to God because as the Creator of heaven and earth, He alone is the source of inexhaustible power, unconditional love, and acceptance. He knows the number of hairs on your head! Psalms 139:17–18 (NIV) says, "How precious to me are your thoughts, God! How vast is the sum of them! Were I to count them, they would outnumber the grains of sand-- when I awake, I am still with you." It is hard to understand the magnitude of God, but He has continually shown Him to be trustworthy to me. All people tend to attach their cord to someone or something. You may not have put much thought in who or what you decide is worthy of your trust, but underneath it all, there is something.

The LORD does not look at the things people look at. People look at the outward appearance, but the LORD looks at the heart.
—1 Samuel 16:7b (NIV)

You have searched me, LORD,
and you know me.
You know when I sit and when I rise;
you perceive my thoughts from afar.

You discern my going out and my lying down;
you are familiar with all my ways.
Before a word is on my tongue
you, LORD, know it completely.
You hem me in behind and before,
and you lay your hand upon me.
Such knowledge is too wonderful for me,
too lofty for me to attain.
Where can I go from your Spirit?
Where can I flee from your presence?
If I go up to the heavens, you are there;
if I make my bed in the depths, you are there.
If I rise on the wings of the dawn,
if I settle on the far side of the sea,
even there your hand will guide me,
your right hand will hold me fast.
If I say, "Surely the darkness will hide me
and the light become night around me,"
even the darkness will not be dark to you;
the night will shine like the day,
for darkness is as light to you.
For you created my inmost being;
you knit me together in my mother's womb.
I praise you because I am fearfully and wonderfully made;
your works are wonderful,
I know that full well.
My frame was not hidden from you
when I was made in the secret place,
when I was woven together in the depths of the earth.
Your eyes saw my unformed body;
all the days ordained for me were written in your book
before one of them came to be.
How precious to me are your thoughts, God!
How vast is the sum of them!

Were I to count them,
they would outnumber the grains of sand—
when I awake, I am still with you.
— Psalm 139:1–18 (NIV)

The LORD is good to those whose hope is in him,
to the one who seeks him;
it is good to wait quietly
for the salvation of the LORD.
—Lamentations 3:25–26 (NIV)

The LORD is my light and my salvation—
whom shall I fear?
The LORD is the stronghold of my life—
of whom shall I be afraid.
— Psalm 27:1 (NIV)

Now the Lord is the Spirit, and where the
Spirit of the Lord is, there is freedom.
—2 Corinthians 3:17 (NIV)

CHAPTER 5

Why Remember?

*Vision is the ability to see God's presence, to perceive God's
power, to focus on God's plan in spite of the obstacles.*
—CHARLES R. SWINDOLL

L ast year I had the privilege of visiting and praying with a lady
who had lung cancer that had spread into her bones. This lovely
lady was in so much pain in her bones. I hurt for her. As I was sitting
there listening to her, God reminded me of a time I had been in pain
like that and how He had removed it. I had not thought about my
pain leaving for several years and had basically forgotten the pain
unless I strained my shoulder or hip. How does a person forget?
I don't have the answers, but I guess it is like when women have
babies. It hurts a lot, but we forget and carry on until the next baby
comes along and then ask, "Was I crazy?"

My bones had started hurting before I was diagnosed with
cancer for the second time. My shoulder, arm, and pelvis would
ache. I had gone to my family doctor for x-rays. Nothing showed
up, and he suggested losing some weight. I lost quite a bit of
weight but the pain kept getting worse, and eventually my glands
began to swell. The pain was just a nagging pain at times, but
other times there was this awful gnawing that would keep me
up at night. One night I hurt bad. By then I knew my cancer had
returned for the second time. Radiation would help the pain, but

I chose to opt out as radiation can only be used once on an area. I was concerned that if the chemo did not work, I would need radiation more later on if the cancer continued to spread. I lay in bed crying as it hurt. I pleaded with God to give me strength to cope with the pain or to remove it. I prayed through the night as the pain lessened and finally left. The areas were still tender to touch, but the pain never came back. God heard my cry to Him to intervene on my behalf. He came to help and removed my pain. He is a God who hears.

Later when I visited with this lady, I remembered the pain God had removed. I could relate to the following story. The Bible tells the story of the Israelites and how Moses led them out of captivity in Egypt to finally live in Canaan, the Promised Land. This journey of over forty years took them from slaves to conquerors. They walked across the Red Sea on dry land, and they got water from a rock. Food was provided each day for them. The Israelites wandered for forty years, but their clothes and shoes did not wear out. Sadly, they only remembered what they did not have and what they left behind in Egypt, where they had been slaves. They forgot to be thankful for what was given. The people would cry out to God for help, and the Lord would step in and save the people with mighty acts. The people would worship the Lord until they forgot all He had done for them and His mighty power of their behalf. They would just remember or focus on what they did not have. Psalm 78:42 (NIV) says, "They did not remember his power." They would complain, but when troubles came, they were quick to cry out to the Lord to save them. The pattern continued even after Israel lived in Canaan and carried on through books in the Old Testament.

I could never understand how Israel could turn their backs on God after He had repeatedly performed miracles on their behalf. I used to question how they could forget. Now I could humbly relate as I had quickly forgotten my bone pain. This story is summarized in Psalm 78:105–106. When I went to bed that evening, the bone pain I hadn't had in several years returned in my pelvis and down my leg worse than it had been before. I had just completed a bone scan a few months before, so I was pretty certain the cancer was not raging now in my bones but that it was an attack of the enemy. I went into a room by myself that night to pray. God laid it on my heart to memorize Psalm 91, which is a prayer of protection. I slowly worked on memorizing the verses and claiming them out loud as promises. It is such a great Psalm to remember when in trouble. I finally got all the verses learned and was amazed I was able to remember them. By morning the pain left again and has not returned. Another answer to prayer.

We are no different than the Israelites. We can remember wrongs done to us, hurts, and hardships easily. They circulate around and around in our minds in a never-ending litany. We can convince ourselves that we will never be happy again because of it. You can substitute what you are struggling with. Sometimes circumstances are beyond our control. I can't make my cancer go away, but I can choose to go on and try to find the joy God has in store for me. I do not want to overlook or ignore all the good around. I continue to celebrate the over forty-three hundred days I have been alive since cancer arrived rather than worry about how little time I may have left. I do not want to live in a negative mind-set of lost hopes and dreams. We do not want our circumstances to determine who we are and our happiness. How we choose to live our lives is a choice. The road that we journey down in not always easy and not always of our choosing. It may look like wholeness is beyond reach, but that is a lie. Wholeness will probably look different and may contain cracks, but all things are possible with God. Our cracks and dents are just ways for God's love to shine through for all the world to see.

A friend of mine had moved away just before I found out I had cancer the first time. We used to e-mail back and forth. We would pray and encourage each other, though I seemed to be the recipient of most of the prayers at that time. A few years after I completed my first treatments, Jane stopped for a visit and brought me a gift.

She had kept all the e-mails we had written back and forth. She had put them in a binder so I would always remember the goodness of God. I sat down and read so many good things that I had forgotten about. One e-mail was about a time I was getting anxious to get on with treatments as I had waited so long. I had found the first cancer at Christmas, and this was May. I had asked Jane to pray for things to get started. A few days later, I e-mailed back and told her how I was heading to the hospital to meet the chemo nurse to go over procedures and would start treatment the next day. I had been home recuperating from a lumpectomy. The phone rang, and the nurse was overjoyed as she had phoned twenty-five people to find someone to start treatment because of an unexpected opening. I was the first one to answer the phone. Coincidence? I say it was God hearing and answering our prayers.

Another friend, Sheila, shared with me her stones of remembrance. On her coffee table sits a bowl of random stones. She records on a stone each time God answers special prayers or intervenes in her life in a remarkable way. She keeps them there so she does not forget. She loves sharing a story or two if anyone asks about the stones. She called them her stones of remembrance, which is where the title of my book comes from. I want to be able to share with my daughters and my grandchildren the mighty acts of God on my behalf. I do not want them to forget how God walked with me. The one who walks each day with me wants to have the same relationships with my daughters or anyone who calls out to Him.

Sheila got the idea for her stones from the story of Joshua leading the Israelites across the Jordan River. The people had crossed the river on dry ground because the waters from upstream had stopped flowing as soon as the priests carrying the ark of the covenant touched the water. Joshua 4:4-8 (NIV) explains,

> So Joshua called together the twelve men he had
> appointed from the Israelites, one from each

tribe and said to them, "Go over before the ark of the LORD your God into the middle of the Jordan. Each of you is to take up a stone on his shoulder, according to the number of the tribes of the Israelites, to serve as a sign among you. In the future, when your children ask you, 'What do these stones mean?' tell them that the flow of the Jordan was cut off before the ark of the covenant of the LORD. When it crossed the Jordan, the waters of the Jordan were cut off. These stones are to be a memorial to the people of Israel forever. So the Israelites did as Joshua commanded them. They took twelve stones from the middle of the Jordan, according to the number of the tribes of the Israelites, as the LORD had told Joshua; and they carried them over with them to their camp, where they put them down."

The stones were stacked up as stones of remembrance. He did not want the people to forget.

I encourage you to find a way to remember your celebrations and successes. Recording something positive will force you to keep looking for the positives each day. We then have a journal to pull out and remember the good on the days we hit a wall or stumble. The journal or stones of remembrance will encourage you to step out again and not give up. Find your own way of remembering, whether it is a journal, a mural, a poem or whatever works for you, but do it. Your stones will keep calling you back to important truths. The truth that God is always with us, loves us, and works mightily on our behalf. We never want to forget. Stones of remembrance encourage us to carry on with a heart full of gratitude for all that God has done for us. What stones of remembrance from your past make you grateful, build your faith, guide your steps, and occupy your mind?

Whoever dwells in the shelter of the Most High
will rest in the shadow of the Almighty.
I will say of the LORD, "He is my refuge and my fortress,
my God, in whom I trust."
Surely he will save you
from the fowler's snare
and from the deadly pestilence.
He will cover you with his feathers,
and under his wings you will find refuge;
his faithfulness will be your shield and rampart.
You will not fear the terror of night,
nor the arrow that flies by day,
nor the pestilence that stalks in the darkness,
nor the plague that destroys at midday.
A thousand may fall at your side,
ten thousand at your right hand,
but it will not come near you.
You will only observe with your eyes
and see the punishment of the wicked.
If you say, "The LORD is my refuge,"
and you make the Most High your dwelling,
no harm will overtake you,
no disaster will come near your tent.
For he will command his angels concerning you
to guard you in all your ways;
they will lift you up in their hands,
so that you will not strike your foot against a stone.
You will tread on the lion and the cobra;
you will trample the great lion and the serpent.
"Because he loves me," says the LORD, "I will rescue him;
I will protect him, for he acknowledges my name.
He will call on me, and I will answer him;
I will be with him in trouble,
I will deliver him and honor him.

With long life I will satisfy him
and show him my salvation.
—Psalm 91 (NIV)

Hear my cry, O God;
listen to my prayer.
From the ends of the earth I call to you,
I call as my heart grows faint;
lead me to the rock that is higher than I.
For you have been my refuge,
a strong tower against the foe.
I long to dwell in your tent forever
and take refuge in the shelter.
—Psalm 61:1–4 (NIV)

CHAPTER 6

Calming the Storms

*If you allow it, [suffering] can be the means by
which God brings you His greatest blessings.*
—CHARLES R. SWINDOLL

Life returned to normal in many ways after my first confrontation
with cancer. I found that I looked at priorities differently but life
carried on. I returned to work as soon as I returned from radiation.
I was supposed to have Herceptin treatments for a year but had to
quit after a few rounds. Teaching was exhausting with my heart
problems, but I needed routine in my life.

One day, about seven years after my first run-in with cancer, I
noticed a large swollen gland on my neck, which seemed strange as
I felt healthy except my aching bones. I ignored it for several days,
and then other glands started popping out. I went to my doctor, who
confirmed that my cancer had likely returned and spread. Many
procedures, scans, and tests over the next few months confirmed
that the breast cancer had returned and had metastasized to my
bones and throughout my lymph system. The oncologist concluded
that they could try to slow down the cancer, but it could not be
cured. It was terminal, and I was given one to six years to live. Not
what I wanted to hear. I had known that the original breast cancer
may return, but I had hoped and prayed that I would be one of the

lucky who that walked away—one who got to let cancer fade into a distant memory. God had other plans for my life.

Did you ever enjoy the game of tug-of-war? I loved being part of a tug-of-war match as a kid and on sports day while I was teaching. I love cheering and competing in a match. The teams would appear even until one team started to tire or someone tripped and one team would start to slowly give way to the opponents. Have you ever had a tug-of-war with God? That is what it felt like over the ensuing months of tests and waiting. I could accept that God was in control and knew that while this cancer did not come from God, He had in His wisdom allowed it to return again, but I still wanted my way, my life, and not what He was asking of me. It sounds so foolish, but I am sure all of us have done this at some time or another. I would pray for healing, which would be so easy for God. God would counter with Psalm 46:10 (NIV), "Be still, and know that I am God; I will be exalted among the nations, I will be exalted in the earth." This verse was beginning to sound very familiar.

I truly believe that God not only loves us continually but also has the power to heal. I must admit that I just knew or wanted to know that the final test results would be negative. I would be healed so I could share God's goodness with others. God did meet with me and totally healed me, but not in the way I wanted or expected. Instead, He continued to change me. The Lord's ways and thoughts are not ours. The following passage from Isaiah 55:8–9 was constantly brought to mind: "'For my thoughts are not your thoughts, neither are your ways my ways,' declares the LORD. 'As the heavens are higher than the earth, so are my ways higher than your ways and my thoughts than your thoughts'" (NIV). I knew in my heart that God was trying to tell me to trust Him no matter what the results were and to continue to trust in Him when I could not understand everything, but I still kept praying for the cancer to leave *now*.

I would pray and claim the verse from Jeremiah 17:14 (NIV), "Heal me, LORD, and I will be healed; save me and I will be saved, for you are the one I praise." God would show me how He was healing my heart and calming my soul in the midst of my circumstances. He would whisper words of encouragement and love into my heart, reminding me of His continued presence. I pored over the Psalms of David. Every time David feared or struggled, he would run to God and call out to Him, waiting expectantly for an answer. He had such faith and trust in God. David was far from a perfect man, just as we are far from perfect. The Lord never asked for King David or anyone to be perfect but rather to love Him with all our heart and soul. God loves and accepts us right where we are.

This story shows a tug-of-war King David had to change God's mind. King David had stayed home instead of going out to fight with his army and ended up having an affair with Bathsheba, who was married to a soldier, Uriah the Hittite. As a soldier, Uriah was out fighting for the king. Bathsheba became pregnant, and David tried in many ways to cover up his actions but to no avail. Finally the king sent a letter to Joab, the leader of his army, and said, "Put Uriah in the front line where the fighting is the fiercest. Then withdraw from him so he will be struck down and die." After the time of mourning was completed for Uriah, David married Bathsheba. She had a son.

David thought he had covered up his past but forgot that God sees and knows all things. The Lord sent the prophet Nathan with a message to the king. Nathan chastised the king for what he had done. His message from God was that there would be consequences for the evil David had done. David finally asked God to forgive his immorality and the murder of Uriah. David's plea is recorded: "Do no cast me away from Your presence, do not take Your Holy Spirit from me." from Psalm 51:11 (NIV), shows that his humbling desire to be in the presence of God made David a "man after God's own heart." God forgave the king as He does with us. This time, though, Nathan said there would be consequences for his vile actions. David got to choose which consequence, and David chose that his new son would die. The Bible says the king chose that because he hoped the

Lord still might hear his prayers and let the boy live. Verse 16 says, "David pleaded with God for the child. He fasted and went into his house and spent the nights lying on the ground. The elders of his household stood beside him to get him up from the ground, but he refused, and he would not any food with them." The story above comes from 2 Samuel 12 (NIV).

Seven days later the child of David and Bathsheba died. "Then David got up from the ground. After he had washed, put on lotions and changed his clothes, he went into the house of the Lord and worshiped." The servants could not understand his actions. He answered them in verse 22, "While the child was still alive, I fasted and wept. I thought, 'who knows? The Lord may be gracious to me and let the child live.' But now that he is dead, why should I fast? Can I bring him back again? I will go to him, but he will not return to me."

I played the tug-of-war game with God much like David did in hoping that God would be gracious and remove the cancer. I would cry out to God because I might never be able to see my daughters get married or hold my grandchildren. God would send verses like Joshua 1:9 (NIV) that kept me going: "Have I not commanded you? Be strong and courageous. Do not be afraid; do not be discouraged, for the LORD your God will be with you wherever you go." Another verse being Deuteronomy 31:6 (NIV), "Be strong and courageous. Do not be afraid or terrified because of them, for the LORD your God goes with you; he will never leave you nor forsake you." These verses would be given to encourage me. As a side note, I have since danced at two of my daughters' weddings and had the delight of loving my four granddaughters. He continues to show me His grace and answers my prayers. I am still praying to make my last daughter's wedding!

Once the cancer was diagnosed, it was time for me to accept my journey and get on with life. I am slow at times, but God was definitely showing me that though the struggles ahead might be unsettling, He would be with me continually. I slowly gave up tugging on the rope. Tug-a-war with God does not make a winner or loser. Giving up our perceived rights and desires to God does not mean losing. It is actually stepping over the center line to be on God's side so that now you can battle beside God rather than against Him. A wonderful peace came over me the day I accepted my circumstances. I was ready, with God's strength, for treatments. The Lord has promised that if He permits a challenge in our life, He will definitely provide the grace to carry on.

The oncologist explained the drugs I would be on for treatment. Herceptin was one. I had needed to go off this drug years earlier because it had caused damage to my heart muscles and almost put me into heart failure after a few rounds. Over time my heart had slowly recovered most of my heart functions. Now doctors were telling me to not only take this drug during treatment but for the rest of my life. My thoughts were, *No way! How is this going to work?* To take Herceptin meant probable heart failure, and to not take it meant dying of cancer soon. Not a good choice. Take the drug or not? I did not like either choice, but again God reminded me of 2 Timothy 1:7 (KJV), "For God hath not given us the spirit of fear, but of power and of love and of a sound mind." I decided I had to give the drug another try and leave the rest in God's hands rather than cowering in fear.

I love it that when we call out to God, He answers. His answers are not always in the way we expect, but He reassures us that He is there and is in control. God answered my prayers in two ways before my chemo treatments started. First I was given a vision or dream to encourage me. I saw this vision while praying and reading my Bible. I was out in a barren field with a huge storm rolling in over the horizon. The storm was howling and racing toward me. Great funnels of tornados were stretching down all around me. I could feel the power of the storm and wind pulling at me. I felt the terror of being swept away in one of these monstrous funnels as they rushed toward me. It was hard to breathe. I could not move. One funnel came right over me and started to descend, but nothing happened! It came partway down, but it did not rip me apart. I finally looked up and realized I was in the center of the funnel, and there was Jesus above me, smiling down on me with His arms outstretched. It was beautiful. There was quietness, warmth, and peace. I looked at Jesus and felt such overwhelming love and peace. When I glanced sideways at the funnel surrounding me, I could feel the wind distort my body and try to pull me back into the storm. The wind quit ripping at me the instant I looked back at Jesus. He told me to just keep my eyes fixed on Him and He would take care of the storm.

I felt a calm over my thoughts. Jesus was teaching me how to survive whatever was ahead. When anxiety or poor results came in, I could see Jesus reaching down to comfort and calm me. Jesus is so worthy of praise and glory. The storms in my life had not changed, but I learned to put my hope and trust in Jesus as I went forward from there. I kept my eyes on Jesus, and He dealt with the storms. I was safe in His care. He is and always will be more than enough for any storm.

But we have this treasure in jars of clay to show that this all-surpassing power is from God and not from us. We are hard pressed on every side, but not crushed; perplexed, but not in despair; persecuted, but not abandoned; struck down, but not destroyed. ... Therefore we do not lose heart. Though outwardly we are wasting away, yet inwardly we are being renewed day by day. For our light and momentary troubles are achieving for us an eternal glory that far outweighs them all. So we fix our eyes not on what is seen, but on what is unseen, since what is seen is temporary, but what is unseen is eternal.
—2 Corinthians 4:7–9, 16–18 (NIV)

God is our refuge and strength,
an ever-present help in trouble.
Therefore we will not fear, though the earth give way

and the mountains fall into the heart of the sea,
though its waters roar and foam
and the mountains quake with their surging.
There is a river whose streams make glad the city of God,
the holy place where the Most High dwells.
God is within her, she will not fall;
God will help her at break of day.
— Psalm 46:1–5 (NIV)

CHAPTER 7

Golden Thread

*The pursuit of happiness is a matter of choice ... it is
a positive attitude we choose to express. It is not a gift
delivered to our door each morning, nor does it come through
the window. And it is certain that our circumstances
are not the things that make us joyful. If we wait for
them to get just right, we will never laugh again.*

—CHARLES R. SWINDOLL

It was time to start my second go at chemotherapy. I was to
have one new drug and two that I had used before. God sent
some wonderful ladies to pray and encourage me before starting.
I love how God reached out to encourage me through my love
of sewing. I enjoy sewing or making quilts and decided to start
a fresh, new quilt as a means of distraction. Sewing would keep
my mind and hands busy while I was weak from treatments. I cut
out all the pieces and started sewing. One morning my machine
kept jamming, and every single seam I sewed was wrong. I was so
frustrated that I threw the pieces on the floor, stomped on them,
and kicked them into a corner. This is my typical response when
frustrated with sewing. Not very grown up, but it sadly makes me
feel so much better. With the pieces heaped in a corner, I decided to
go to prayer time at our church. God was definitely working while
I was busy having a hissy fit.

One of the ladies, Claire, stopped while praying for me and asked if I enjoyed sewing as she kept seeing a vision of tiny pieces of black and white fabric with all these patterns. She went on to describe some of the patterns that were exactly what I was using on my quilt. I explained to her that I did sew and was actually working on a black and white quilt that used many of the patterns she described. I didn't tell her that the pieces were wadded up in a corner and that was why I ended up coming for prayer that day! God told her that just as I was sewing all those pieces together to create something beautiful, God also was sewing pieces, all the pieces of my life together to create something beautiful. The difference was that God was sewing all the pieces of my life together with golden thread that could never be broken. Unlike quilt seams that rip over time or have to be torn apart to fix mistakes, what God creates or mends in us is perfect. She went on to say that God wanted me to make this quilt and to praise and worship Him while I was making it and to remember that He was at work in me. I left the prayer room that day praising God. My cancer hadn't changed. I still had to somehow take this drug that had caused my heart problems, but I knew God would be with me through what lay ahead. God was creating something beautiful in my brokenness that only He could do. What an amazing promise of what He wants to do in each person's life.

I felt reassured that whatever was ahead, I knew God would be working in and through my life to create something beautiful. Don't you love how He said He would be creating something beautiful rather than "average." Beautiful! I kind of felt like a caterpillar struggling to get out of my cocoon to see what God was going to create. That day I fell before God in brokenness and ashes, but He began the process of creating something new and good, which He still continues to this day. The words of the song "Something Beautiful" by William Gaither poured from my heart:

Something beautiful, something good;
All my confusion He understood.
All I had to offer Him was brokenness and strife,
But He made something beautiful of my life.

I stopped on the way home and bought spools of brilliant gold thread that I used to sew every single seam on that black and white quilt. My golden seams that I made on my quilt will someday wear out, but the seams God continues to piece together in my life are permanent. I praise God for sending a message to me that day. He showed me how He keeps His promise of never leaving or forsaking me. He gives the same promise to any person who calls out to Him.

It may seem like an odd task for God to give me, but I felt whole inside sewing that quilt for God. I knew in my heart that God would be there with me when sewing or stepping out in faith during treatments. I did a lot of praying, worshipping, and listening to God as I sewed. Philippians 4:4–9 (NIV) meant a lot to me:

Rejoice in the Lord always. I will say it again: Rejoice! Let your gentleness be evident to all. The Lord is near. Do not be anxious about anything, but in every situation, by prayer and petition, with thanksgiving, present your requests to God. And the peace of God, which transcends all understanding, will guard your hearts and your minds in Christ Jesus. Finally, brothers and sisters, whatever is true, whatever is noble, whatever is right, whatever is pure, whatever is lovely, whatever is admirable—if anything is excellent or praiseworthy—think about such things. Whatever you have learned or received or heard from me, or seen in me—put it into practice. And the God of peace will be with you.

The quilt now graces a bed in my home. I love to go and look at it and be reminded of what God has done and continues to do in my life. This quilt is one of my stones of remembrance. I have shared my cancer quilt and the story of God's promises with so many people. I always cry when I tell the story, and so do most people when they hear of God's provision and great love. As you walk through your struggles, may you declare Psalm 107:1 (NIV) along with me: "Give thanks to the LORD, for he is good; his love endures forever."

I put many hours into finishing the quilt after I retrieved it from the corner and started over yet again. This time I praised and worshipped the Lord in praise and meditated on God's Word as I sewed and was drawn closer and closer into His arms of love. I do not think of the time, labor, or how many seams I had to rip out, but I love the beauty and warmth of the completed project. This is the same way that God works in and through us if we allow Him. Sewing is like what God is doing in our lives every day. He takes bits and pieces of our ordinary lives and creates something beautiful when we allow Him to. The Lord wants to create something lasting and sturdy in us that will not deteriorate or fall apart with use and time. He often ignores the flashy and flimsy that may be appealing to us but instead creates a masterpiece that endures the test of time. As we allow the Holy Spirit to work freely in our lives, He stitches our joys and tears together to make you the person our Maker created us to be. He sees everything in you, loves you, and wants to sew the tiny bits of scrap together into something even more beautiful. Are you willing to let the Holy Spirit work in you, or are you going to demand your way as you clumsily try to sew the pieces together by yourself.

This story of my cancer quilt reminds me of the verse in Isaiah 64:8 (NIV), which is about the potter and the clay. "Yet you, LORD, are our Father. We are the clay, you are the potter; we are all the work of your hand." Circumstances can break us, and we do not know how to mend our broken lives enough to carry on. We hurt, tremble in fear, and feel lost. We wonder if we can ever fix our problems or circumstances. God tells us that it is His job to mend our brokenness because He is the potter and we are the clay. The clay does not make the pot or bowl by itself. It is the job of the potter. Jesus is our potter. He sees the broken pieces, cracks, or tears in our lives that hurt and defeat us. He watches us trying to remake our lives whole again by ourselves. He hurts along with us but patiently waits for us to ask Him to help us fix the brokenness. Jesus is a gentleman and never pushes Himself into our lives. He quietly whispers in our hearts that He loves us and waits for us to invite Him to come in and heal us. His desire is as the potter's; He wants us whole.

Japanese artisans have practiced the craft of kintsugi, which means golden joinery or to patch with gold. These artisans put broken shards of pottery back together using gold and lacquer. These artisans transform broken ordinary pottery into stunning works of art. The goal is not to mend or restore the seams to be hidden but to fill the breaks with gold. The once-broken shards are better than new. The broken seams now glow with gold light just like the seams that God wants to sew our lives together with. The golden seams are stunning and change an ordinary piece of pottery, or an ordinary person, into a masterpiece. This is what God wants to do in our lives. He alone can mend our hearts and put back the broken pieces of our lives back together to make something beautiful. Out of the rip or hurt that breaks our life, God desires to create a masterpiece of great worth and value that glows for all to see. It is like my cancer quilt. God said that He was sewing the pieces of my life together with golden thread that could not be broken. God was and is creating something beautiful in my life just as He wants to do in your life.

My job was to learn to rely on God to mend the hurts, fears, and cracks as He is the potter. I was to worship Him through my journey, make my quilt, and carry on with life. Each day God continues to put pieces of my life together to make "beauty from ashes," and He wants to do the same for each of us. We need to daily remind ourselves that our attitude toward what God has allowed into our lives needs to be pleasing to Him. We may not understand why something is happening or how long it will continue or even what the end results will be, but the Lord knows. We step out in trust and faith and let God do the rest. His grace is always sufficient for whatever comes at us.

> Therefore, since we have been made right in God's sight by faith, we have peace with God because of what Jesus Christ our Lord has done for us. Because of our faith, Christ has brought us into this place of undeserved privilege where we now stand, and we confidently and joyfully look forward to sharing God's glory. We can rejoice, too, when we run into problems and trials, for we know that they help us develop endurance and endurance produces character, and character produces hope, And this hope will not lead to disappointment. For we know how dearly God loves us, because he has given us the Holy Spirit to fill our hearts with his love.
> (Romans 5:1–5 NLT)

> But he said to me, "My grace is sufficient for you,
> for my power is made perfect in weakness."
> Therefore I will boast all the more gladly about my weaknesses,
> so that Christ's power may rest on me.
> —2 Corinthians 12:9 (NIV)

> I can do all this through him who gives me strength.
> —Philippians 4:13 (NIV)

> You have searched me, Lord,
> and you know me.

You know when I sit and when I rise;
you perceive my thoughts from afar.
You discern my going out and my lying down;
you are familiar with all my ways.
Before a word is on my tongue
you, Lord, know it completely.
You hem me in behind and before,
and you lay your hand upon me.
Such knowledge is too wonderful for me,
too lofty for me to attain.
Where can I go from your Spirit?
Where can I flee from your presence?
If I go up to the heavens, you are there;
if I make my bed in the depths, you are there.
If I rise on the wings of the dawn,
if I settle on the far side of the sea,
even there your hand will guide me,
your right hand will hold me fast.
If I say, "Surely the darkness will hide me
and the light become night around me,"
even the darkness will not be dark to you;
the night will shine like the day,
for darkness is as light to you.
For you created my inmost being;
you knit me together in my mother's womb.
I praise you because I am fearfully and wonderfully made;
your works are wonderful,
I know that full well.
My frame was not hidden from you
when I was made in the secret place,
when I was woven together in the depths of the earth.
Your eyes saw my unformed body;
all the days ordained for me were written in your book
before one of them came to be.

How precious to me are your thoughts, God!
How vast is the sum of them!
Were I to count them,
they would outnumber the grains of sand—
when I awake, I am still with you.
—Psalm 139:1–18 (NIV)

CHAPTER 8

The Storm

It's the most exciting thing to watch God work when I've asked
him about something, to listen to him and watch him work. It's like
this friendship, and it just grows and grows and grows and grows.
—CHARLES SWINDOLL

There is nothing like watching giant thunderheads roll in on a hot summer day. You can feel it in the air as you watch the clouds roll in. The thunderheads are magnificent as you see the huge anvil-shaped clouds start to form in the distance. The wind starts blowing as the storm creeps even closer. You can feel the pressure in the air, and everything is hot and muggy. Then the rumbling starts. Lightning flashes, and finally the rain pours. I never tire of watching storms, usually from the safety of our carport. The clouds pass, the rain peters out, and the air smells fresh and clean. Last, a rainbow appears to let us know that God is there reminding us of His promise to never flood the whole earth again. Our daughters loved to run out into the rain as soon as the lightning passed so they could puddle jump. Their shrieks of laughter filled the air. They would eventually trudge in soaking wet, wanting a cup of hot chocolate. Happy memories.

I don't enjoy getting caught out in thunderstorms without cover or protection. My view of a storm is different when I can't get to safety. The same can happen in our lives when storms arrive to wreak havoc in our lives. We often feel helpless when circumstances are out of our control. You can probably relate to storms that occur in your life. You can see the clouds building but hope and pray that the lightning passes you by. If you are like me, you do not want to have to deal with the effects of storms. Storms have a way of turning our lives upside down, and we are left wondering, *What is going on?* This is how I felt when I went through my second set of chemotherapy.

My side effects were minimal the first time going through cancer. The second time was a different story. I told you earlier one of the three drugs I was to take was Herceptin, which had caused me many heart problems. I started treatment but quickly began to demonstrate side effects from Herceptin but also from one of the other drugs I needed to take. I was told that a few people may lose some feeling in their fingers or feet by the end of treatments. The night of my first, treatment I sat with pins and needles in my hands, both feet, up my right leg, and right up to the top of my head. A numbness replaced the pins and needles by morning and lasted three or four days. This same problem arose after each subsequent treatment but lasted longer. Each time more of the numbness stayed. I would just sit and try to ignore what was happening and ask God give me the strength to cope. Over the next few years, most of the numbness left, but I still have some numbness in the tips of my fingers, between my toes, and in the bottoms of my feet.

The verse that kept running through my mind was Isaiah 48:18 (NIV): "If only you had paid attention to my commands, your peace would have been like a river, your righteousness like the waves of the sea." I love this verse of God's promise of peace. I love that God offers peace like a river. Rivers always change and are never stagnant. They are filled with life and change with each season. Rivers twist and turn so you don't always know what is ahead around the next corner. I used to think of peace as a static and life had to be calm to have peace. I slowly learned that our destination or circumstances do not define peace. Peace came from keeping my eyes on Jesus and letting God deal with the side effects. I grew up near a river and spent countless hours swimming, fishing, tubing, or just sitting and watching the river flow peacefully by. The peace of God moves and fills us as it flows in and through us like a river. Peace like a river is forever moving as it brings new, fresh life. When we stay close to God, then His peace runs through us like a river. Our peace runs dry when we disconnect from our source, which is God. A river will also run dry if the tributary is blocked or cut off. We need to be daily fed from God so our peace can flow like a river to sustain us.

The treatments became more challenging as time went on. During this time, I was part of a ladies' prayer group. The friendship, laughter, love, and prayers of those women were like air to me. They surrounded me in their love. They stood by me and encouraged me to stand on the promises of God. They believed even when my faith would falter. They pushed me on. They helped me to lay all my worries at the feet of our Lord and let Him fight the battle that was beyond my capabilities. They were warriors on my behalf, and I will always be grateful for them and the multitude of others who surrounded me and still do. If you are in the midst of a struggle, I urge you to find someone to walk with you as these wonderful women and friends did with me.

I had completed only two or three cycles of chemo when my heart started to have problems. My heart functions fell to 32 percent, and my heart was going into arrhythmia. I had to take a break from the drugs. This is when God showed me a vision of a trail while praying. I was out in a meadow enjoying the sun and the grass. Glancing up, I noticed a flash of light from the forest that surrounded me. I went over to investigate and noticed a small trail. I started following it into the trees. The trees were sparse at the beginning but got thicker and thicker as the trail wound on. It became quite shaded and was hard to find which way to go at times. I would decide to turn around when I would notice another glimpse of light ahead. I knew inside me that there was something special about the light even though I couldn't see where it was coming from. I knew I was supposed to follow the light. The trail started to climb up an incline. I began to tire, but the light would glow each time I felt too exhausted to continue. The light would illuminate the trail when I was feeling lost or unsure. The path became very steep, and eventually I was above the tree line. I looked ahead and saw that the trail led up the side of a cliff face ahead. The path was getting extremely narrow. The valley was far, far below.

With my heart pounding, I wanted to go back to the meadow where I came from but I couldn't turn around on the ledge as it was too narrow. I searched for handholds to cling to as I took tentative steps forward. The light was shining steady now, and it seemed to be coming from behind a huge rock at the top of the path. I knew inside that I had to make it to the light. Pieces of path were crumbling under my feet, and I could hear them falling to the valley below. I was so scared as I hugged the face of the mountain, inching forward. I was frightened to look at anything but the light shining from around the rock ahead. Finally arriving at the rock, I scooted around it, and there was light glowing everywhere. It was beautiful. There was a meadow with a river running through it. Jesus was standing by a small waterfall with His hand reaching out to me. He was so happy to see me, and I felt so loved. I never wanted to leave. Jesus believed that I would make it up that mountain! We had a great time of celebration and danced for joy.

I prayed about the vision and felt that Jesus was telling to keep on going with my treatments even when it seemed hopeless, dangerous, and at times frightening. I felt that I was to following the light, which was Jesus, who would show me the way. I was to keep my eyes focused on Jesus and His promises, and I would get through. Jesus would be there holding my hand and leading me each step along the way. He would surround me with His light to guide me, encourage me, and rejoice with me at the end, whether we would celebrate here or in heaven. God did not tell me if I would make it through chemo or if I would go to be with Him. He just said

He would show me the path to follow. This bothered me at first, but I decided that following Jesus was my only choice. Jesus wanted me to step out in faith and follow His leading. I would hold onto that vision and the promise that Jesus was with me each step when side effects became so hard and all I wanted to do was to turn and run. I would hold onto Jesus' hand and make baby steps forward even when common sense told me that my body was rejecting the chemo.

This reminds me of the story of Moses leading the children of Israel out of Egypt to camp by the Red Sea. Pharaoh had let the people of Israel leave but changed his mind when he realized that all his slaves were gone. Exodus 14:10–14 (NIV):

> As Pharaoh approached, the Israelites looked up, and there were the Egyptians, marching after them. They were terrified and cried out to the Lord. They said to Moses, "Was it because there were no graves in Egypt that you brought us to the desert to die? What have you done to us by bringing us out of Egypt? Didn't we say to you in Egypt, 'Leave us alone; let us serve the Egyptians'? It would have been better for us to serve the Egyptians than to die in the desert!" Moses answered the people, "Do not be afraid. Stand firm and you will see the deliverance the LORD will bring you today. The Egyptians you see today you will never see again. The LORD will fight for you; you need only to be still."

The children of Israel of given up all hope and feared facing the vast Egyptian army and all its chariots. They thought all was lost. They cried out to the Lord but never dreamed that God would come to their rescue in such a dramatic way. As Moses stretched his staff over the waters, the Red Sea parted, and the Israelites crossed over on dry ground. The cloud that led the people moved behind them but in front of the Egyptians until all of Israel had crossed the Red Sea. God answers when we ask but in such amazing ways. Cross the sea on dry ground? Who would think of such a solution? The Egyptians tried to catch Moses and the people. They set out to cross the sea between the towering water banks. The walls collapsed and drowned the Egyptians. Many people do not believe in miracles such as these. Several years ago an archeological dig thought they had found the remains of the chariots and the army while searching for something else at the bottom of the Red Sea. The archeological remains are there to retell the story of God's deliverance.

I did carry on with treatment by faith, though I must admit there was much trembling on my part. The light of Jesus went with me to show me the way so I did not lose hope or make wrong decisions. The vision gave me confidence instead of making me fearful. Jesus promises His grace and strength for each day. We are at times faced with obstacles we are incapable of overcoming on our own. We fear ending up broken and wrecked. It is when we call out to Jesus that grace arrives to do what we can't do on our own. Grace is God meeting us right where we are at and giving us all, as in everything, we need to get through. We call out to Jesus, and He surrounds us with His care, not because we are good enough, strong enough, or have more faith, but because He loves each and every one of us. It is God meeting and loving us right where we are and offering to take our burdens upon His shoulders. I will again repeat 1 Peter 5:7 (NIV), "Cast all your anxiety on him because he cares for you." Jesus then fights our battle as we step out in trust and faith to obey and follow His leading.

This vision of me following the light up the mountain reminds me of the apostle Paul when he was on his way to Rome to stand trial. God had told Paul that he was being sent to Rome to tell the good news that Jesus was the Messiah but that it would bring hardships. Paul was on his way to Rome as a prisoner, not because he had done wrong but because he had preached that Jesus was the risen Messiah. The Jews in Jerusalem wanted to kill him, but because he was a Roman citizen, he was sent to Rome for a trial before Caesar. Though in chains, Paul preached the risen Lord until the day he died. He knew in his heart that he was being sent by God to Rome to tell others of Jesus so would not be deterred. He did not want to go in chains, but he went anyway. Paul says in Acts 20:23–24 (NIV), "I only know that in every city the Holy Spirit warns me that prison and hardships are facing me. However, I consider my life worth nothing to me; my only aim is to finish the race and complete the task the Lord Jesus has given me—the task of testifying to the good news of God's grace."

The ship that Paul was aboard kept encountering difficulties on its way to Rome. It was getting late in the season for sailing, but the owners wanted to go on instead of staying in harbor. The Holy Spirit had warned Paul that there would be disaster if they set off, but the ship's captain and owners wanted to carry on. In Acts 27:10 (NIV), Paul warned them, "Men, I can see that our voyage is going to be disastrous and bring great loss to ship and cargo, and to our own lives also." Money won out, and they set sail. They encountered a hurricane as Paul had predicted. The ship floundered for a few weeks and finally ran aground on an island. All aboard survived.

Paul was in chains and shipwrecked but never gave up hope because in his heart he was being sent by God to Rome to tell others of Jesus. He had a task to complete, and nothing was going to stop him. He focused on the task set before him and left the rest in the Lord's hands. He believed that a shipwreck wouldn't stop him if God wanted him in Rome. He lived his life and did not let fear or the unknown stop him.

Paul probably felt like we do when trials loom on the horizon. We try to avoid them or search for an easier way. The question I have for you, and ultimately also myself, is, are we willing to step out in faith as Paul did, even when we know it will be hard and painful? Will we take cover and hide from the storm on the horizon, or will we trust God to walk with us? Will we cut and run, or will we, like Paul, be able to say in Philippians 4:13 (NIV), "I can do all this through him who gives me strength." You will fall on your face multiple times if you are like me. The beauty of grace is that every time we fall, Jesus comes and dusts us off and helps us get back on our way. His grace never fails or runs out. He goes with us because Jesus knows we can make it if we hold onto His hand.

A friend once shared Psalm 30:5 (NIV) with me: "For his anger lasts only a moment, but his favor lasts a lifetime; weeping may stay for the night, but rejoicing comes in the morning." We can hold onto that promise that even if we may weep for a while, rejoicing will come in the morning. We just need to hold onto our hope and the promises that God gives. Joy will come in the morning. When the morning arrives, we will still be standing. Isaiah 61:1–3 (NIV) tells us that Jesus came to bind up the brokenhearted and walk with us so we can become oaks of righteousness—strong, full of life, and the person we were created to be.

> The Spirit of the Sovereign Lord is on me, because the Lord has anointed me to proclaim good news to the poor. He has sent me to bind up the brokenhearted, to proclaim freedom for the captives and release from darkness for the prisoners, to proclaim the year of the Lord's favor and the day of vengeance of our God, to comfort all who mourn, and provide for those who grieve in Zion— to bestow on them a crown of beauty instead of ashes, the oil of joy instead of mourning, and a garment of praise instead of a spirit of despair. They will be called oaks of righteousness, a planting of the Lord for the display of his splendor. (Isaiah 61:1–3 NIV)

A giant oak, full of life, splendor, strong, and beautiful. May we all grow to be like that as we allow Jesus work in and through our lives.

The following Psalm reminds us to lift up our eyes to see the one from where our help comes from. Our God never sleeps nor slumbers but walks with us each and every step of our journey if we allow Him to. The journey may be hard, but He is there with you and loves you with an everlasting love. He promises to never leave nor forsake you. Take this journey with Jesus, learn of Him, cling to His promises, and let Him create something beautiful in your life.

> I lift up my eyes to the mountains—
> where does my help come from?
> My help comes from the Lord,
> the Maker of heaven and earth.
> He will not let your foot slip—
> he who watches over you will not slumber;
> indeed, he who watches over Israel
> will neither slumber nor sleep.
> The Lord watches over you—
> the Lord is your shade at your right hand;
> the sun will not harm you by day,
> nor the moon by night.
> The Lord will keep you from all harm—
> he will watch over your life;
> the Lord will watch over your coming and going
> both now and forevermore.
> — Psalm 121 (NIV)

Finally, be strong in the Lord and in his mighty power. Put on the full armor of God, so that you can take your stand against the devil's schemes. For our struggle is not against flesh and blood, but against the rulers, against the authorities, against the powers of this dark world and against the spiritual forces of evil in the heavenly realms. Therefore put on the full armor of God, so that when the day of evil comes, you may be able to stand your ground, and after you have done everything, to stand.

—Ephesians 6:10–13 (NIV)

CHAPTER 9

Fears and Doubts

Because God gave you your makeup and superintended
every moment of your past, including all the hardship, pain,
and struggles, He wants to use your words in a unique
manner. No one else can speak through your vocal cords,
and, equally important, no one else has your story.

—CHARLES SWINDOLL

Our enemy, Satan, loves to whisper lies in our minds that fill
us with fear and doubts. The lies twist the truth and make
us doubt all we know of God. The Bible tells us that the enemy
must flee when we call upon the name of Jesus, but sometimes it's
not easy to recognize the lies. James 4:7 (NIV) tells us, "Submit
yourselves, then, to God. Resist the devil, and he will flee from
you." I was attacked by the enemy when I was at my weakest during
a break from treatment when my heart was going crazy from the
chemo. I had never encountered such a spiritual or physical attack.
I let fear consume me, which opened the doors for doubts to pour
in. The Lord fought the battle for me and won a great victory. Trust
me, I was too weak and overwhelmed to do more than just hold
onto the mighty right hand of God.

Someone loving came to visit and encourage me one day. She
had the best intentions. In trying to help me, she explained that my
cancer should be gone since Jesus had healed everyone who asked

in the Bible. This meant that Jesus had to heal me *if* I had enough faith—the big "if," as if my faith or lack of it changes who God is or what His purposes are. She gave me a short book that would explain the concept in more detail and asked me to read it. The book was all based on Isaiah 53:5 (NIV), which says, "But he was pierced for our transgressions, he was crushed for our iniquities; the punishment that brought us peace was on him, and by his wounds we are healed." This wonderful verse was used to prove the author's point that I was full of cancer only because of my lack of faith.

The author continued to say that a person could be healed one day, but if his or her faith slipped below some invisible line that only God knows, the sickness would return. Thankfully, this is not how the God of grace treats people. God and the grace He freely gives is so much bigger than our minds can even begin to comprehend.

I tell this story to illustrate how the enemy takes fears, good intentions, and weaknesses and twists them to try and destroy us. I gave room for the lies to grow in my fear instead of casting them out in Jesus's name.

Jesus was crushed and pierced and I am healed, as Isaiah says. Jesus does heal everyone who comes to Him in prayer, but the healing will occur on God's timeline during this life or in heaven. We think of healing through our eyes, and we can only see the here and now. We can't understand the big picture that God sees, as He looks at our circumstances from heaven's view. He would never remove His healing or grace from us, but He may decide to take us home to be with Him.

Without grace, we miss out on what God desires to do in our lives and we instead demand our own way. We may not always understand why something happens. We may never understand while we are on earth. God's ways are not always ours. Isaiah 55:8 says, "'For my thoughts are not your thoughts, neither are your ways my ways,' declares the Lord." We also find in Romans 11:34, "Who has known the mind of the Lord? Or who has been his counselor?"

Psalm 116:15 (NIV) says, "Precious in the sight of the Lord is the death of his faithful servants." God loves us so much that He sent Jesus to die on the cross so we could live with God in heaven. He does not ignore the prayers of His people for healing. We are precious in His sight.

Psalm 139:16 (NIV) tells us, "Your eyes saw my unformed body; all the days ordained for me were written in your book before one of them came to be." Our days are already numbered, so sickness can never shorten the days God has given us, yet God longs for us to be with Him in heaven, where there is no sickness or tears, and we will go there when our days are finished.

He heals our bodies on His timeline, but He always heals our hearts and gives us the privilege of being called children of God. We have been made whole because of what Jesus accomplished on the cross and the grace He freely shares. Grace is free. It is not works, nor is His grace ever withdrawn if our faith wavers.

Healing is more than the temporary removal of our physical problems. The Lord heals brokenness, hurts, loneliness, and desolation. The list could go on forever. Healing can be either instantaneous or a slow process. Some people think God is obligated to do what is demanded of Him on our timelines. We can't see life through heaven's eyes and perceive all the purposes of God, but we can stand on His promises and know that He loves us and only wants the best for us. God's thoughts and purposes are not always ours.

I totally knew that the book given to me was not right, but it still planted seeds of doubt in my mind. That is not how God works thankfully. Ephesians 2:8–9 (NIV) says, "For it is by grace you have been saved, through faith—and this is not from yourselves, it is the gift of God— not by works, so that no one can boast." We are saved or healed by God's grace alone, never by works or our amount of faith.

Another example that explains this is found in Mark 17:17–29. A man had brought his son to Jesus to be healed. The boy had battled with seizures since childhood. The father says to Jesus, "But if you can do anything, take pity on us and help us." The man didn't even know if Jesus was able to heal the boy or not. He was asking Jesus as a last resort after years of trying to help his son. The man did not even understand that Jesus was the Son of God. He just knew that some guy had come to town and was doing miracles and healing people. Jesus did not turn the man away. I love verses 23–24 in the Living Version, which tells of their conversation. "What do you mean, 'If I can'?" Jesus asked. "Anything is possible if a person believes." The father instantly cried out, "I do believe, but help me overcome my unbelief!" The son was healed, not because the father had enough faith for a miracle but because he called to Jesus. It was grace, not works, and certainly not the amount of faith the father had.

We also know of the story of the apostle Paul, who had a thorn in the flesh that was never fully described but thought to be some kind of eye problem. He called out to God three times begging for healing but was told no. Second Corinthians 12:8–9 says (NIV), "Three times I pleaded with the Lord to take it away from me. But he said to me, 'My grace is sufficient for you, for my power is made perfect in weakness.' Therefore I will boast all the more gladly about my weaknesses, so that Christ's power may rest on me." If anyone had unshakable faith, it was Paul. Paul accepted God's will was more important than the healing of his problem during his life time. This "thorn in his flesh" made Paul learn to rely on Jesus. Ultimately, we all need God's grace if we are going to accomplish the calling God has given for each one of us. Our calling is far greater than our own abilities, so we need to learn to rely on grace. It is a learning process.

I think of two great women who have accomplished so much with their lives in spite of their disabilities that God has allowed. Joni Erickson Tada broke her neck as a teenager while diving. She is a living testimony of how a person can live a vibrant, useful life in spite of circumstances. She speaks continually of God's grace.

She writes books, does radio shows, paints, sings, and much more. She has made such an impact on others from a wheelchair and paralyzed from the neck down. She has allowed God to use her for His glory.

Another woman, Michelle Perry, has lived an amazing life even after being born with one leg. She is unstoppable. She ran an orphanage in Sudan. This woman amazed me with her faith in her book *Love Does*, as she survived everything from rebel forces to sharing God's love to people in a war-torn country. These women have prayed for healing but have accepted their lives as they are. They both believe they have a purpose and are allowing God to use them in unbelievable ways just as they are. Both of their stories are inspiring to read about.

God does heal people, but He does it in His way, in His timing, and for His glory. We can bring praise and honor to our heavenly Father through healing or in sickness by relying on the strength and grace of God to carry on. Who am I to tell God what or when to do something? He alone knows the future and what He is working on in my life to bring Him glory. I love Romans 8:28 (NIV): "And we know that in all things God works for the good of those who love him, who have been called according to his purpose." The point isn't only about instantaneous healing but rather God working in and through our lives to create something beautiful inside each of us. Yes, I would rather be totally be healed of cancer and continue to pray for this. At this point God has shown me great grace, healing, strength, and courage daily that I would never have experienced if I had never walked this cancer road for over forty-three hundred days. We live in a world surrounded by people, and if my life and struggles encourage others step out and turn to Jesus, I can live with cancer.

Now on with the story. On the day of the spiritual attack, I was so weak and sick that I could not walk without assistance or leaning against a wall. I was about halfway through treatments in my second kick at cancer. My heart had crashed. One drug was causing my heart to go into arrhythmia, and the Herceptin was damaging the muscles pumping the blood. My heart was functioning at 32 percent and beating erratically. The doctors sent me home for a month or more to give my heart a rest. I was a wreck to say the least. It is at times like these, physically and mentally beat, that the deceiver loves to come with lies aimed at destroying us. First Peter 5:8 says, "Be alert and of sober mind. Your enemy the devil prowls around like a roaring lion looking for someone to devour."

I was totally overwhelmed by the thought of needing to get back to chemo, knowing how weak my heart was. The enemy had been attacking my mind over the last months, telling me that I was a disappointment to God and that was why my cancer had come back. All I could see was what I could not do. I felt like I was a disappointment to my family, my friends, doctors, and God because my body was not strong enough to be able to deal with the drugs. The disappoint routine was something I had struggled with for a long time. I knew the lies were not true, but I couldn't stop the litany that constantly circulated through my mind. "Loser," is all I could think. This is when I was given the book that I described above. Thankfully, I have come to know a God of love. In my heart, I knew that God is not petty or spiteful as the book portrayed, but my thoughts kept the repeating loop of, *Maybe I am not only a disappointment but also lack enough faith to be helped by God. Why should God listen to such a pitiful person?* It got worse and worse, and I felt like I was losing my mind. All I could do was to call out to Jesus for help. I could not go on. I was defeated, flat out on my face. I had hit a brick wall. I went to bed broken and cried myself to sleep.

God works in such wondrous ways. The Lord saw my weakness and sent a message to me through a friend in India. Julie, a delightful friend of one of my daughters, was in India working with YWAM. God spoke to Julie asking her to pray for me as I needed it badly. God also gave her a verse to send to me. Don't you love how God works? I opened my e-mail the next morning, and there was this message that steered me back to God and wholeness. Julie wrote,

"I was praying for you tonight as you were heavy on my heart. God told me He gave you a crown of glory, beauty, and wisdom. He also gave me this verse for you, and we all gathered to pray for you." Can you believe these young people on the other side of the world bowed down and were praying for me when I was so broken? There aren't word to explain how loved I felt. How often have we heard God asking us to pray for someone but put it off? I do not do that anymore. Anyway, they prayed, and this is the verse Julie sent. Philippians 4:4–7 (NIV) says,

> Rejoice in the Lord always; again I will say, rejoice! Let your gentle spirit be known to all men. The Lord is near. Be anxious for nothing, but in everything by prayer and supplication with thanksgiving let your requests be made known to God. And the peace of God, which surpasses all comprehension, will guard your hearts and your minds in Christ Jesus.

I slowly began to praise God for this message of hope and asked God to show me how to fight off this attack.

This was not a fast process, nor was it easy to break out rejoicing with praise as the verse said. This took every single bit of discipline and energy I had. I felt like I was in the battle of my life, but I did not want to stay where I was. I determined to not believe the lies but asked God to show me who I was as His child. He did. As I read the Bible, I would say His promises out loud and claim them each time my heart would start to beat erratically or the discouraging thoughts came. I sat there all day claiming God's promises, and finally as it was getting toward evening, wonderful peace came and filled the cracks in my heart. Peace flooded my heart like a healing balm. I felt exhausted but whole and free again. The Holy Spirit kept reminding me of the vision He had given me of keeping my eyes of Jesus and leaving the rest to God, which included all the heart problems. I couldn't fix my heart, but I could face the future with confidence and peace. I was free to worship Jesus and rejoice. Later on attacks would come, but I had memorized the promises of God and the enemy would flee as soon as I began speaking the promises aloud.

By evening I felt surrounded by God's love. I felt as if God had pulled me onto His lap and wrapped His arms around me. I was sitting there safe, bathed in His healing light and love. He whispered promises of love and encouragement until I was strong enough to walk on my own by holding tightly to His hand so His light could show the trail ahead. I felt as if I had been in the fight of my life, for my very existence, my faith, and my sanity but now had an overwhelming sense of peace because, with the help of God, I had confronted my worst fears and doubts. God had met me, not with condemnation for my lack of faith but with love. Our doubts and fears do not make God any less. He is more than capable of showing anyone who He is if we but ask Him. By evening I was physically and mentally exhausted but whole and free again.

God was not finished encouraging me in my battle. I went to church the next Sunday. I was weak and shaky, but everything in me told me to go. My husband helped me get there as I could not go on my own. My husband is always early for everything, so he arrived maybe twenty minutes early when the prayer warriors were praying. They called me over to pray. I had asked them to pray for my heart so I could get on with treatment. Now remember how I explained that I was struggling with being a disappointment to God and everyone. Wait till you hear what God wanted me to know. If fact, He wants all of us to know this. We had a guest speaker that morning, and he came over and grabbed my hand out of the blue. He said that God had given him a message for me. I had never met or talked to this man, nor can I tell you his name! He said, "God wants you to know that you are not a disappointment to Him. In fact, God has never been disappointed in you." Wow! I was blown away again. The man then went on to say that he was supposed to pray for the healing of my liver. I was in pain in the area of my liver but had not said anything. I was waiting for a MRI scan to see if the cancer had spread to my liver. It had looked suspicious in a CT scan, but the doctors said the image was not totally clear. He prayed, and the pain in the area of my liver left and has never returned. The MRI scan also came back clear eventually! Isn't it amazing how God reaches out to us to love and restore us even when we are too weak to have faith or the strength to stand on our own?

God had one more miracle for me a few weeks later. I was leaving a worship concert when Claire, a powerful prayer warrior, stopped me and said she felt that she was to pray for me. She asked me what was going on. I told her that I had to start back on chemo in two days but was unsure if my heart could take it. Claire started praying and then stopped. She said that as she was praying, she could see Jesus wielding a paint brush as He painted my heart white. Jesus was using a brush to paint both the inside and the outside of my heart to protect it from the drugs. My mind was blown. I had been praying for wisdom but love how God answers prayers in such unusual ways.

Chemo day arrived, and I had to decide whether to trust God and go ahead with my heart or quit and run. I took a baby step and asked Jesus to keep painting my heart in extremely thick coats and coats of paint and went ahead with treatment. I was able to go on and complete all the cycles of treatment. I understand the fear that Peter must have felt as he stuck his foot over the side of the boat to walk out to Jesus on the water! The treatments were not easy, but my heart seemed to settle down a bit even though I was still using the same drugs and dosages as before. I finished! The doctors tested my heart when I finished and found that my heart was functioning normally. Now that was a miracle! I was able to continue on with Herceptin every three weeks for almost four years with no heart issues.

I meet with a doctor at the cancer unit every three weeks for blood work and a checkup. This was because I was still taking doses of Herceptin. Last year I met the doctor who had treated me while I was going through the initial chemo when my heart crashed. She checked me over and then said she was amazed at how well I was doing. She recalled when we had discussed continuing with treatment when the outlook was so grim. She told me that she had not been able to write out the orders for treatment when I resumed my chemo because she did not think I would make it. She made the oncologist write the orders. Yes, it was God who blew us all away. He wields one miraculous paint brush.

You may be reading this and thinking that God would never do that for you. Just call out to Jesus and let Him amaze you. Jesus said in Matthew 11:28 (NIV), "Come to me, all you who are weary and burdened, and I will give you rest." We live in a fallen world and should expect troubles, but we do not have to be defeated. You may fall flat many times, but God is always there to pick us up, dust us off, and get us back on our journey when we ask. We always have the choice of how we face obstacles. One choice is calling out to Jesus and standing on God's powerful promises. Prayer moves mountains. Rejoice in the Lord, as my friend from India reminded me, and focus your mind on what is good. Philippians 4:8 (NIV) says, "Finally, brothers and sisters, whatever is true, whatever is noble, whatever is right, whatever is pure, whatever is lovely, whatever is admirable—if anything is excellent or praiseworthy— think about such things."

I will exalt you, Lord,
for you lifted me out of the depths
and did not let my enemies gloat over me.
Lord my God, I called to you for help,
and you healed me.
You, Lord, brought me up from the realm of the dead;
you spared me from going down to the pit.
Sing the praises of the Lord, you his faithful people;
praise his holy name.

For his anger lasts only a moment,
but his favor lasts a lifetime;
weeping may stay for the night,
but rejoicing comes in the morning.
When I felt secure, I said,
"I will never be shaken."
Lord, when you favored me,
you made my royal mountain stand firm;
but when you hid your face,
I was dismayed.
To you, Lord, I called;
to the Lord I cried for mercy:
"What is gained if I am silenced,
if I go down to the pit?
Will the dust praise you?
Will it proclaim your faithfulness?
Hear, Lord, and be merciful to me;
Lord, be my help."
You turned my wailing into dancing;
you removed my sackcloth and clothed me with joy,
that my heart may sing your praises and not be silent.
Lord my God, I will praise you forever.
—Psalm 30 (NIV)

Forget the former things;
do not dwell on the past.
See, I am doing a new thing!
Now it springs up; do you not perceive it?
I am making a way in the wilderness
and streams in the wasteland.
—Isaiah 43:18–19 (NIV)

CHAPTER 10

The Bell

*Learning more truth is a poor and cheap substitute for
stopping and putting into action the truth already learned.*
— CHARLES R. SWINDOLL

*The heart is deceitful above all things and
beyond cure. Who can understand it?*
—JEREMIAH 17:9 (NIV)

There is a bell that hangs on the wall in the chemo room. Patients get to ring this bell when all their rounds of chemo are completed. They ring the bell with such glee and joy. Chemo is finished, and life can carry on. I hate that bell. I know that sounds foolish, but I really, really, really hate that bell. The doctors told me the second time my breast cancer returned that it had metastasized to my bones and lymph system and so it was incurable. I will never get to ring it unless God chooses to do a miracle. Instead I sit in the chemo room and stare at the bell and smile when others ring it. Some days I want to take the bell and throw it out the closest window, and other times it takes all I have to not go up and ring it and ring it some more. I am not sure if I would be ringing it in hope or defiance. Such foolishness, but I hate hearing that bell ring. I smile, cheer, and clap when someone else rings the bell, but inside I hurt. The bell makes me angry, and I sit and ask God why. Why not me? Why? I am sure that everyone can relate to something in their life they have wanted to do so badly but can't. It may be a foolish desire, but it is part of who we are.

I am generally a happy person and enjoy the accomplishments and joys of others. What does surprise me at times is the anger, envy, and hurt that can swamp me when I hear that annoying bell ring. In my head I want to be happy for the person but not always in my heart. Several people I know have also faced cancer over the last few years. They have gone through the tests or treatments and all has come out fine. Part of me rejoices for them, but there is a small part of my heart that hurts and questions why God has provided healing for them but not me.

I do not want to think about the anger because it is hard to admit that my heart can be so ugly. I wanted to be truly happy and thankful along with these people. Many women I know have had breast cancer like I have. I see them, and their cancer has not returned. They seem to go merrily on with life as if they have no cares. Without a miracle, I never will.

At first I ignored the feelings and convinced myself I was being silly, but I was angry and hurt. I was angry at God. I was angry that these people were fine and I wasn't. Yikes. When people share their wonderful news of being cancer free, I think of the long, dark tunnel ahead of me. More drugs, more tests, more scans, more, more, and just more pain. It will only stop when I leave this place to meet Jesus. The anger brings more questions. God, why do You heal some people but not me? God do You love these people more than me? What have I done to deserve this? Why? Why? Why? It is not fair. I hate myself for feeling like this.

Each time I would ask God why, He would answer with 2 Corinthians 12:9 (NIV): "But he said to me, 'My grace is sufficient for you, for my power is made perfect in weakness.' Therefore I will boast all the more gladly about my weaknesses, so that Christ's power may rest on me." I may be a little slow at times, but I finally realized that God was answering my cry but just not how I expected or wanted. God's answer was that His grace would be enough for whatever lay ahead. I had the choice to accept that this was the road that God had laid out for me to walk for now or to sit and continue feeling sorry for myself. Not accepting the journey God has for me is a useless waste of time and would only open a door to bitterness that I do not in my life.

With the help of Jesus, I began to stop comparing my experience to others. Each person has his or her own trials as well as blessings. One person's life is not better than the another's, but each is different. Comparing my circumstances to others' circumstances leads to anger and envy. In reality I have no idea what other people are facing beyond the small glimpse they allow me or anyone else to see. For all I know, I may be envying foolishness. How can I compare my "insides," my thoughts and feelings, with someone else's outside? We can't see the "insides" of those around us.

People are usually good at remembering all the hard trials endured. These negative thoughts just love to circulate in a never-ending litany in our minds. If we let these thoughts continue, we stop seeing and being thankful for all the blessings that surround us. We overlook the beauty and love we are given each day. Envy makes us blind to all the good. We always want more or what someone else has. I read a quote once that went something like, "Unhappy people are usually ones with ungrateful hearts. No matter what they are given, it is never enough because they feel they deserve more." I never want to be like that.

Each time the envy and anger would arise, God would show me verses to reassure and comfort me. Here are a few. Isaiah 41:10–13 (NIV) says:

> Fear not, for I am with you; be not dismayed, for I am your God; I will strengthen you, I will help you, I will uphold you with my righteous right hand. Behold, all who are incensed against you [I put my cancer as the one against me] shall be put

to shame and confounded; those who strive against you shall be as nothing and shall perish. You shall seek those who contend with you, but you shall not find them; those who war against you shall be as nothing at all. For I, the Lord your God, hold your right hand; it is I who say to you, "Fear not, I am the one who helps you."

Matthew 28:20b (NIV) constantly runs through my mind when the anger or hurts come: "And surely I am with you always, to the very end of the age." Again, there is no answer to why but a promise, and my heart is at peace because Jesus is always close beside me.

Joshua 1:9 (NIV) is on my heart through the day and night. "Have I not commanded you? Be strong and courageous. Do not be frightened, and do not be dismayed, for the Lord your God is with you wherever you go."

Deuteronomy 31:8 (NIV) says, "It is the Lord who goes before you. He will be with you; he will not leave you or forsake you. Do not fear or be dismayed."

Jeremiah 31:3 (NIV) says, " The LORD appeared to us in the past, saying: 'I have loved you with an everlasting love; I have drawn you with unfailing kindness.'" These promises kept reassuring me that God was always with me, hadn't forgotten me, and loved me. I need the constant reminding.

God is so gracious and loving. The anger and hurt I felt were not a secret from Him. He knew each time I ached or was filled with anger. He knew I resented others for appearing to be healthy and carefree. It is not what we want to admit, but God knows our every thought and loves us completely. He never condemns us for the anger and envy but reassures us of His continued love and presence. Then the Lord shows us a better way—a way that brings peace rather than letting us destroy ourselves with our negative thoughts.

Have you ever felt like this? The people around you appear to have an easy life and your heart is breaking or your life is falling apart. It feels like a giant weight is sitting on your chest crushing all the life out of you. This does not have to be a health issue to feel like this. These feelings also arise in our homes, workplaces, with friends, or from loss. I may not understand your circumstances, but I can relate to a broken heart. There is never a heart so broken that God can't heal it. Many of the problems we face can come from our own poor lifestyle or decisions, but many are out of our control and they just happen. Either way is never a surprise to God. He is always there when we call out to Him. God loves us in spite of our choices or circumstances. He just wants us to reach out to know Him. He comes with love, acceptance, and strength, never condemnation as we often tell ourselves.

The Bible is so full of stories that help us deal with our emotions. I have marveled that such an ancient text is still so emotionally relevant. King David wanted to build a temple for God. David had built several beautiful palaces in Jerusalem when he became king of Israel. David wanted to build the temple to demonstrate his love and devotion for the Lord, his Creator and friend. The Israelites used a tent as a temple that they had made while in the desert. The Lord told David that he was not to build the temple but instead, David's son, Solomon, was to construct it. The reason given was that David had been a man of war and had shed much blood. If you read about the wars and battles of David, you can see that he was a mighty warrior. When eventually Solomon reigned, all was peaceful in Israel.

David could have chosen to be angry over God's decision. I am sure he felt some disappointment and envy. Instead, David got busy designing and getting supplies gathered so everything would be ready when Solomon was ready to build. David made a positive choice. He could have defied God and built the temple anyway, or he could have whined and complained. David worked to ensure that the actual construction of the temple would be ready and also easier for Solomon. He chose to glorify his Lord in any way he could. He gathered cedar and pine trees. He set aside huge quantities of gold, silver, and bronze. He worked for the good even though David knew that he would never see the finished product. He would never ring the bell! Sounds familiar, doesn't it?

It is not the whys we need to know but the who. David knew; the who is Jesus. God said no and David accepted the verdict because God had proved to David that He was worthy of his trust. The days of our lives are already known and numbered. I cannot change the number of days I live. None of us can say how long we will live, whether we ring the bell or not. Our days are held in God's hands. I can choose how I live those days. I can choose to be angry, resentful, and afraid or thankful for each day, one at a time. Every person has their own journey to follow in this life. We have different journeys, but they are all held in the loving hands of our Lord, who promises to never leave or forsake us. God's grace is abundantly sufficient for all our needs, and His love all encompassing.

God loves us so much that He looks beyond the ugly in our hearts and sees the person we can become with His help. He loves and accepts us the way we are but also loves us enough to only want the best for each of us. I may not know all the whys until I meet Jesus face to face. Until that day, I will hold onto the who, which is more important. The who is forever, Jesus. I may not know all the answers, but I do know who has earned my trust over and over again. The Lord is walking with me and holding my hand. He can see the whole picture and understands all the whys. I put my whys and my trust in the Lord as He has never let me down.

Someday I will meet my friend Jesus, and together will ring that bell. I'll ring it and ring it and ring it again because there will be no sickness, no pain, no heartache. I will be healed, not for a short time like here on earth, but for eternity. Maybe we can meet up, and we'll ring the bell together.

I praise you because I am fearfully and wonderfully made;
your works are wonderful,
I know that full well.
My frame was not hidden from you
when I was made in the secret place,
when I was woven together in the depths of the earth.
Your eyes saw my unformed body;
all the days ordained for me were written in your book
before one of them came to be.
How precious to me are your thoughts, God!
How vast is the sum of them!
Were I to count them,
they would outnumber the grains of sand—
when I awake, I am still with you.
— Psalm 139:14–18 (NIV)

Search me, God, and know my heart; test
me and know my anxious thoughts.
See if there is any offensive way in me, and
lead me in the way everlasting.
— Psalm 139:23–24 (NIV)

CHAPTER 11

Friends and Encouragers

I cannot even imagine where I would be today were it not
for that handful of friends who have given me a heart full
of joy. Let's face it, friends make life a lot more fun.
— CHARLES R. SWINDOLL

True friendship one of the greatest gifts a person can have or give. I have been loved on, encouraged, and upheld by such friends. I have learned to appreciate how a simple act of friendship can change the whole day. It does not have to be some grandiose gesture. It can be a smile, a phone call, or a card in the mail that brings enormous joy. Going for a walk with a friend to laugh and chat is like a hidden treasure. A shared laugh brings light to a dark day. I love playing a game of cards while surrounded by people who care. Friends and family have a way of making you feel loved and treasured.

The first time I went through cancer, I had my family and many friends to encourage me. I had just changed churches before I found out I had cancer. We had gone to the same church for years and I was content there, but my daughters were not. They had been asking me to change churches and I had even felt the urging of the Holy Spirit, but I found it difficult to leave. Everything came to a head one Sunday morning, and my daughters stood up and said they would not return to the church again. They had felt betrayed and hurt, and whether it was true or not, I needed to listen to their hurts, so we left. We started looking around for another church but never quite found a fit for any of us. I got cancer and felt lost without a church family to call home.

After completing chemo and radiation after my first time with cancer, I ran into a friend who invited me to her church. It was a fairly new church and I thought it was worth the try. Have you ever had the feeling that you have finally come home? That is how I felt the day I walked in. I belonged. The next times when cancer returned, I had a church family that has encouraged me with love and prayer.

Spending time with friends has always been important to me. I remember having no immunity for months during flu season during my second time through chemo. Somebody would phone and want to stop by for tea. They would later have to cancel due to coughs or flu. Even my wonderful grandkids were constantly sick. I think I drove my husband crazy. A woman has to get a certain number of words in each day, and he had the only available ears! I love being with people and meeting new ones. People fill my cup. I could fill a book with stories of all the love poured out to me from so many people and in such a variety of ways. The Bible says in Proverbs 17:17 (NIV), "A friend loves at all times, and a brother is born for adversity." This is so true! Proverbs 18:24 (NIV) puts it this way: "One who has unreliable friends soon comes to ruin, but there is a friend who sticks closer than a brother."

My friends have been valuable throughout my journey with cancer. Each friend has his or her own way of showing care. Some would phone and make me giggle. Others would offer powerful prayers. Others would cook a meal. Some friends would stop for tea. Others would arrive and get me out for a walk. Some offered advice, and a few just told me what to do! I have several friends that remind me of Proverbs 27:17 (NIV), "As iron sharpens iron, so one person sharpens another." My friend Linda, who is a nurse, continually questions my health decisions and how I take care of myself. She cares enough to tell me when I am being foolish. She stands up to me and makes me think about my choices. She speaks her mind and sharpens my mind in turn. I appreciate her. Another friend, Sheila, pushes me to chase after God. She loves to pose questions that make my mind really think. I spend weeks after talking to her searching the Bible for answers to her questions. I have been privileged to meet the mighty prayer warriors from the Healing Rooms in town. These women offer powerful prayers and encouragement to all that come. They have prayed for me and encouraged to wait with expectancy for God to answer prayers. They have also encouraged me to stand on the promises of God.

Some people have disappeared from my life at times. They have a hard time seeing disease and pain right in your face. It makes them uncomfortable, and they need space. You notice the "deer in the headlights" expression when they first see you. It used to hurt when someone would ignore me or say a quick hello and quickly exit, but I can understand their unease now. Seeing people suffering great loss or being very sick can be unsettling. They may not be ready to confront dying or sickness yet or simply do not know what to say or how to reach out. I used to feel like that at times when I was clueless about what to say. The example of friends has taught me to just be there for others who are hurting. It can be as easy as giving a hug and a smile. Reaching out to someone who is hurting does not mean you have to have all the answers. No one expects you to. You just need to show up and show that you care. Listen or make someone laugh. Hold someone who is hurting. Pray for that person and really pray, not just say you are going to. My friends have shown me how to respond to a hurting world. You just show up.

All of us have probably been asked to look at a glass and see whether if it is half full or half empty. The visual I prefer to use is just a glass. It does not really matter how much is in the glass. The task is to carry it out at your side. The glass is light, and it appears to be an easy job. How about if you were asked to hold the glass out for a long time? What was easy at the beginning starts to feel heavy.

Eventually, your arms start to ache, and the glass feels unbelievably heavy. The longer you hold it out, the heavier it becomes. Your arms tremble, then you shake all over trying to hold this glass out. You finally reach the point when you can no longer hold up what used to appear simple. The glass crashes to the floor.

Problems, trials, loss, health issues, or whatever burden we carry become heavy and overwhelming over time, like this glass illustration. The ache becomes too much to bear on our own. That is when we need not only friends and family but Jesus. He wants to walk with you and be your friend and help carry your load. In Matthew 11:28–29 (NIV) Jesus says, "Come to me, all you who are weary and burdened, and I will give you rest. Take my yoke upon you and learn from me, for I am gentle and humble in heart, and you will find rest for your souls." How often we struggle to carry all our own burdens. The weight that seemed easy at first makes us tired, discouraged, and overwhelmed. We reach our breaking points. Jesus wants us to turn to Him when we first pick up the glass. Let Him carry the burden. Lean into Jesus and He will give you the strength to carry on.

God sends many loving people to also help us hold up our glass. The follow is an actual example of friends holding up a staff for Moses. Exodus 17:8–14 (NIV) tells how Aaron and Hur helped Moses by holding up his arms when Joshua led Israel into battle against the Amalekites.

> The Amalekites came and attacked the Israelites at Rephidim. Moses said to Joshua, "Choose some of our men and go out to fight the Amalekites. Tomorrow I will stand on top of the hill with the staff of God in my hands." So Joshua fought the Amalekites as Moses had ordered, and Moses, Aaron and Hur went to the top of the hill. As long as Moses held up his hands, the Israelites were winning, but whenever he lowered his hands, the

Amalekites were winning. When Moses' hands grew tired, they took a stone and put it under him and he sat on it. Aaron and Hur held his hands up—one on one side, one on the other—so that his hands remained steady till sunset. So Joshua overcame the Amalekite army with the sword.

The battle was won by Moses upholding the staff of God in his hands. The battle was not won by the strength of Moses. When Moses could no longer hold up the staff, Aaron and Hur held his hands up. How often we need this reminder that we do not fight our battles alone. The battle belongs to the Lord. He is fighting the battle for and alongside us. Jesus carries our burdens and sends friends to come alongside. God sent a multitude to walk with me, encourage me, and pray for me. People would just show up when I needed someone to be with me. I remember one day Tammy showed up at my door. She had a van full of kids but was driving by and stopped to give me a hug. She smiled, gave me a hug, and had to run. Short and sweet. My day, which was hard because of being in pain, changed to joy because of her gesture. The load was lighter, and I could go on. I was not alone. Another gift of friendship.

Several years ago, I felt God was asking me to go and visit a coworker of my husband. He was in a care home with ALS, which had progressed very quickly. I did not know Paul well but felt I was supposed to visit him. I kept putting off going to visit because I felt awkward. I didn't know what to say. God kept niggling at me, and I finally said I would go. I was sitting and thinking about when to go and visit Paul when I heard God whisper inside me, "Ten o'clock tomorrow morning!" I guess that was precise enough. I went the next morning to visit. I was nervous and had convinced myself that Paul would not want me there. Paul had to speak through a computer because of the ALS, so conversations were slow. He had this amazing computer that allowed him to spell words out by looking at the letters.

To my surprise, Paul was happy that I had visited and asked me to come back. We shared a good friendship for several years before he passed away this spring. I would usually read aloud from a Max Lucado book to give him something to think about and to encourage his faith. Paul related to the way Lucado explained God.

I now understand why God wanted me to go and visit Paul. Visiting was for both of us. We both needed the friendship and sounding board. Both of us were facing the same giant of dying and leaving our loved ones behind. We related to each other from a different perspective than the other people who lovingly supported him. We could talk about fears, dying, anger, and putting our faith and hope in Jesus. We could have the conversations that often made others uncomfortable. We were both looking at life from a different viewpoint. We had accepted that our time might be shorter, so our perspective had changed. I used to laugh at our conversations. I would ask Paul some simple question, and he would use his eyes to slowly type out a long, expansive explanation. He had lost his ability to speak, but oh, did he have a lot to say. Reaching out to be a friend in need brought both of us innumerable blessings.

Jesus walks with me each day as my strength, my refuge, and my friend. A friend recently questioned me about always referring to Jesus as my friend and the notion that God actually talks to people. She knows the Lord but thought I was a little weird. I love when people ask me questions about hearing from God. I believe God speaks to us through the Holy Spirit, who dwells in us when we come to know Jesus. No, I am not going crazy and hearing voices! It is like a quiet certainty that you hear inside your heart when you are praying, worshipping, reading your Bible, or listening to God. I shared the following words with this lady, who has since gone to be with God.

God spoke to Moses in Exodus 33. God was upset with Israel and said He wanted Moses to lead the Israelites but that God's presence would not go with them. Moses told God that he could not lead Israel without God's presence. God relented and went with Israel because of the request of Moses after they had a discussion!

In fact, Exodus 33:11 says, "The Lord would speak to Moses face to face, as a man speaks with his friend." I used to picture Moses speaking to God, but the Bible says, "God spoke." In Exodus 33:22–23, it sounds like Moses never literally saw God's face but must have come presence to presence with God until his face glowed.

James 2:23 (NIV) says, "And the scripture was fulfilled that says, 'Abraham believed God, and it was credited to him as righteousness,' and he was called God's friend." The Lord met with Abraham and told him what was going to happen to Sodom and Gomorrah. The Lord shared His plans, and Abraham questioned Him. God listened and responded when Abraham asked if the cities could be spared if there were even ten people righteous people found. The Lord agreed that He would spare the city if ten righteous people could be found. You can read of their discussion in Genesis 18–19.

John 15:13–15 (NIV) says, Greater love has no one than this: to lay down one's life for one's friends. You are my friends if you do what I command I no longer call you servants, because a servant does not know his master's business. Instead, I have called you friends, for everything that I learned from my Father I have made known to you." Jesus calls us His friends, so it seems that friendship is not limited to a few mighty men from the Old Testament. Jesus wants to be a friend, so why wouldn't He talk to us through His word or however He wants?

It is so humbling to think that God offers friendship. Amazing! Maybe we just have to make a choice to be more aware and seek out the friendship, listening for His quiet voice. Friendship takes time and effort. Jesus loves us so much and tells us that He wants friendship. Have you been satisfied with the way things are? Have you allowed yourself to become too busy to hear the voice of God calling out to you? I don't have all the answers, but I pray that if God wants to tell me something or longs for my presence that I would intentionally seek Him out with the help of the Holy Spirit and listen. We are seeking to know Jesus as a friend, so why would we limit how He chooses to communicate with us?

But let all who take refuge in you be glad;
let them ever sing for joy.
Spread your protection over them,
that those who love your name may rejoice in you.
Surely, Lord, you bless the righteous;
you surround them with your favor as with a shield.
—Psalm 5:11–12 (NIV)

Bless the Lord, O my soul;
And all that is within me, bless His holy name!
Bless the Lord, O my soul,
And forget not all His benefits:
Who forgives all your iniquities,
Who heals all your diseases,
Who redeems your life from destruction,
Who crowns you with loving-kindness and tender mercies,
Who satisfies your mouth with good things,
So that your youth is renewed like the eagle's.
— Psalm 103:1–5 (NIV)

CHAPTER 12

Courage

Our minds can be kept free of anxiety as we dump
the load of our cares on the Lord in prayer.
—CHARLES SWINDOLL

"Frederick Douglass, the American slave turned social activist, said, 'If there is no struggle, there is no progress.' Your character is formed by the challenges you face and overcome. Your courage grows when your face your fears. Your strength and your faith are built as they are tested in your life experience." The above quote is from the book *Unstoppable* by Nick Vujicic. Vujicic displays his courage for all the world to see daily as he overcomes all odds to live his life out. He is truly unstoppable as he lives a life of joy without the use of arms or legs. His life portrays faith in action. I have heard him speak several times on television as well as having read his book and have been blown away by his positive attitude. He takes joy in whatever he sets out to accomplish with God.

Troubles and personal struggles often cause fear and anxiety, especially when we are facing situations we can't control or fix. None of us enjoy the feelings of betrayal, pain, loss, or brokenness. It is easy to let fear take over when we are in these situations. It takes courage to accept the situation and carry on in spite of the circumstances. What makes two people facing the same situation react so differently? One person faces his or her fears and carries on, hurting but making the best of what he or she is given. The next person crumbles and gives up. There are also people whose fears or regrets have kept them rooted in the same spot even after the struggles have passed. Some people actively relive the pain in their minds each and every day instead of carrying on. They can't let go. People deal with life's pain in widely different ways.

I enjoy visiting with others both in and out of the Cancer Centre and hearing how they face the challenges dealt to them. People are so fascinating. All the stories told are different, but there are similar results. Some people can never say anything positive. They finish the treatments and still live in fear of "what if." Lives are stalled, and issues have never been dealt with. Some avoid fearful thoughts and pretend that all is well and live in a make-believe world. We probably have all used negative coping mechanisms at times when we have faced situations we do not want to deal with. We may be like this while we work through our circumstances initially, but we do not want to stay in this destructive place. I eventually chose to be like the warriors who faced the challenges and just continue fighting with strength, humor, and courage. Each person chooses how to get through struggles. Every day I choose to try to be like the fighters. Some days I fall flat, but with the strength of the Lord, I get up and carry on.

A few years ago I taught a unit on courage with my class at school. The intermediate students were asked to share drawings, sayings, or pictures that showed what courage meant to them. At first all the pictures were of athletes, video game characters, or celebrities. Their accompanying slogans were all about never showing fear or winning at all costs. We put all the ideas up on a wall and decided to add more as our ideas grew or changed. We read and discussed a variety of true stories about ordinary people showing great courage in the face of adversity. The students started to realize that a normal person could be courageous. They read about people who displayed courage in spite of feeling fear or anxiety. Students began to verbalize that courage could be shown in spite of fear. Slowly over the next month or two the students began looking at courage more realistically and realized that everyone has fears and problems. Discussions started to change, and students began to realize that courage was what people did in the face of adversity or fear. Each student read a novel and presented to the class how the main character in the novel faced struggles and difficulties but overcame them with courage. Words like never giving up, keep trying, asking for help, trusting, working together, and accepting what can be changed and what cannot be changed started to be added to our wall. At the end of the unit, the students made posters of real people they thought were courageous. The posters all portrayed ordinary people they knew and admired, like parents, teachers, classmates, friends, or family members. They wrote phrases around the border showing the traits they admired in this person of courage. The class then chose a slogan to show what they learned about courage. Students eventually summarized the unit with this slogan: "Courage is doing what needs to be done in spite of your fears." The students did an amazing job understanding and defining courage.

I used to defeat myself in my own mind when adversity arose. I would allow all the scenarios to go around and around in my mind. It was like walking around the same problem like it was a hill I kept traipsing endlessly around. The problems got bigger as the ruts got deeper and deeper. I would sit and overthink everything, but I wouldn't do anything. The fears grew. I still catch myself doing this at times but am learning to stop and turn to God. A friend reminded me that God gives us the grace and strength to deal with the issues that arise for today only. I would be sitting there worrying about next week or next month rather than dealing with the current day. That is not how God works. He gives us the strength and wisdom for today, not tomorrow. I have learned to ask God what He wants to do or focus on for that day. Tomorrow and the future can rest in God's capable hands.

Trusting God for each day and walking close to the Lord takes time. I had to quit listening to my scenarios in my mind and quit circling the mountain. I would focus on what God was saying. Trusting God was not a one-time decision. It started with small choices each day and throughout the day. It was choosing to not listen to the lies in my head but to open my Bible and read God's promises. It is was a slow procedure of saying no to my thoughts and turning to thank God for what He was doing that day, talking to God, and listening to Him. It was like taking baby steps, but over time my outlook and confidence in God grew and my fears and indecision disappeared.

There is an old movie called *What about Bob?* Bill Murray played Bob, a man who was consumed with fear to the point that his life was a shipwreck. He lived in isolation because his fears kept him house bound. He consulted a psychologist, who gave him a book called *Baby Steps*. Each day Murray would try baby steps to overcome the fears that kept him caged. The movie was very funny but showed how tiny, baby steps made in the right direction can bring about great results. Billy Murray's character slowly gained confidence, and he became free to enjoy life. We can do the same when we stop the cycle of fear and reach out to Jesus. He is ready and willing to use His limitless power for our good. We need to make baby steps toward God.

The enemy wants to tie up our thoughts with fear so we are too overwhelmed to do anything. Jesus said He has come to set us free. Galatians 5:1 (NIV) says, "It is for freedom that Christ has set us free. Stand firm, then, and do not let yourselves be burdened again by a yoke of slavery." Jesus has limitless power, which He wants to use on our behalf if we only ask.

The story of Joshua is a great example of courage. Joshua had been Moses's helper throughout the years coming out of Egypt and wandering in the desert. Moses died, and God told Joshua that he was to be the leader who would take Israel into the Promised Land. Can you imagine having to try to fill Moses's shoes? Moses was a man God used to accomplish amazing miracles. The Bible tells us that Moses spoke face to face to God. He hit a rock that gushed forth with water. Moses raised his staff and stretched his hand over the water of the Red Sea, and it parted for the Israelites to walk through on dry ground. Now Joshua is to lead the Israelites into the Promised Land and defeat the people already residing there. Just a bit of a challenge. We read in the book of Joshua how God told Joshua three times to be strong and courageous. How do we make ourselves strong and courageous? Sounds great, but what steps do we take from fear to courage? God has shown me to trust Him and to make baby steps in the right directions as He leads me.

The first thing I noticed when reading about Joshua was how he totally believed the promises God had given Israel. The plans for the Israelites were the same whether Moses or Joshua was the leader. Joshua 1:1–3 (NIV) says, "After the death of Moses the servant of the LORD, the LORD said to Joshua son of Nun, Moses' aide: 'Moses my servant is dead. Now then, you and all these people, get ready to cross the Jordan River into the land I am about to give to them—to the Israelites. I will give you every place where you set your foot, as I promised Moses.'" Joshua believed what God told him rather than worrying and letting scenarios circle in his head. Joshua's actions showed that he believed God would keep His promises. The Bible tells us that God loves every person and wants only the best for each. The fact that I have cancer does not change how long God has given me to live nor His constant care and love for me. Neither does it change the thoughts or plans He has planned for me. Cancer has not destroyed my life, as I have slowly learned to act on the promises given by God. My life carries on, differently than before, but still a great life.

Joshua believed that God would be with him wherever he went. Joshua 1:5 (NIV) says, "No one will be able to stand against you all the days of your life. As I was with Moses, so I will be with you; I will never leave you nor forsake you." Joshua stepped out in faith because he believed God would always be beside him, which gave him confidence. We can have the same confidence when we confront out battles. God is always beside us, fighting the battles for us. We can know that we are never alone when we step out in faith.

Next Joshua 1:7 (NIV) says, "Be strong and very courageous. Be careful to obey all the law my servant Moses gave you; do not turn from it to the right or to the left, that you may be successful wherever you go." Joshua obeyed God and did not get distracted or choose his own way. Joshua stayed focused and was determined to do only do what God asked. He did not give up when faced with the day-to-day grind of leading the often-reluctant Israelites. He was faithful, and God blessed Joshua and all Israel. Our Lord continues to bless us today as we faithfully follow the course set out for us. It is so easy to get distracted and not spend time with God or to forget about prayer. On our own we make wrong decisions and end up facing problems of our own making. Seeking God's face at the beginning of the day helps with the multitude of small decisions we must make throughout the day. Each little decision is like a baby step.

Last, Joshua started the journey. It sounds obvious, but how many great quests have not been completed because people were too afraid to make the first baby steps? *We defeat ourselves with our thoughts.* We think: *I can't do that. It is too hard. Other people are way more gifted than me. Why try? I will just fail.* Scenarios like these will run through our minds. These depressing thoughts are not of God but from the enemy that wants to defeat us before we even start. Remember, God is with us. Joshua was given a difficult task and got on with the job of leading Israel to cross the Jordan River to the Promised Land. Joshua did not finish the plan in a day, but he made the first step. He assembled Israel and told them to pack up in preparation for crossing the river. Joshua demonstrated his faith by trusting God and starting. Israel crossed the river on dry ground. God did not part the water until the priests carrying the ark stood in the water. Now that takes faith! Israel praised God and went on to march around the walls of Jericho. We all know how the mighty walls fell. Joshua became a great leader to Israel and an example of strength and courage. He believed God's promises are always true. He believed God would go with him and give him the courage and strength to accomplish all that the Lord asked of him. He trusted God, took the baby steps, stepped out and obeyed.

I found walking by faith, step by step, believing that God knew how I was going get through the day became like baby steps—easier each time. Even when I could not see beyond my first tiny step, it was better than doing nothing. If you are struggling with moving forward, you need to throw away the repeating scenarios that swamp your mind. Start today by asking God what the first tiny step is to be, and then ask Him to give you the strength to take your first baby step. He will tell you if you just take the time to listen. Know that God is right there with you in your circumstances. He takes each step with you and never asks more of you than you are able to do with Him. Reach out to Jesus and spend time just soaking in His love. I have been amazed at how my fears run away when I draw near to God. I can feel the strength and comfort of the Holy Spirit girding me up to face the giants. Jesus continually helps me to let go of my fears and lay them at His feet so I can get on with what I am supposed to be doing.

Second Corinthians 5:7 (NIV) says, "For we walk by faith, not by sight." I guess that is what courage is to me: faith. I may not even like or understand all my circumstances, but each day I can make baby steps in the right direction, toward Jesus. What is important is the one in whom I put my trust. Jesus is the one I trust. He will never leave or disappoint me. He provides more courage than needed and fights my disease for me. I try to stay focused on Him and hold onto His mighty right hand that will never let me go. With Jesus, I go from fear to courage to peace. Jesus proved that He really does carry our fears as 1 Peter 5:7 (NIV) says, "Cast all your anxiety on him because he cares for you."

My new favorite song is by Bethel Music called "No Longer Slaves." This song feels like my testimony as I am not longer a slave to fear. It is a beautiful song, and it always makes me cry when I remember how God has replaced the fears I had with peace and joy and surrounded me with His love. I have added a short stanza from the song.

No Longer Slaves
You unravel me with a melody
You surround me with a song
Of deliverance from my enemies
'Til all my fears are gone
I'm no longer a slave to fear
I am a child of God …

I'm no longer a slave to fear
I am a child of God.

Last let's read a promise from Psalm 91:14–16 (NIV) to finish the chapter:

"Because he loves me," says the LORD, "I will rescue him; I will protect him, for he acknowledges my name. He will call on me, and I will answer him; I will be with him in trouble, I will deliver him and honor him. With long life I will satisfy him and show him my salvation."

CHAPTER 13

Brokenness is not the Destination

We cannot change our past. We cannot change the fact that people act in a certain way. We cannot change the inevitable. The only thing we can do is play on the one string we have, and that is our attitude.

—CHARLES SWINDOLL

I am a retired schoolteacher. I loved teaching with all the challenges and the laughter and just being able to spend my days with children. There were challenging days, but I never wanted to do anything else. I loved walking into my classroom each morning and hearing the chatter of young children. It thrilled me to see the excitement in students' eyes when they finally understood something they had struggled with. I even enjoyed the corny jokes! Each year I would ask God to show me something special in each child that He loved about him or her. Through the year I would grow to care so much about each student and get excited to watch them grow and stretch.

I always found September to be a challenge, as most teachers would attest to. Some days were like the survival of the fittest. I, as all teachers, was responsible for creating a safe and stimulating environment for students to learn and thrive. September was a learning time for everyone as we got to know each other and the expectations. Once everyone got on the same page, the job became a joy even though bumps on the road were to be expected. If I were to accept the behaviors, skills, and effort that some students tried at the beginning of the year, little would be accomplished, and everyone would lose out on the pleasure of learning together. I would also be a basket case! If the students or I were to quit and to decide to give up in September, then we would miss out on the best that was yet to come. Challenges did not make me a bad teacher or the students bad kids; it was a time of adjustment and looking ahead to see what we could achieve together. I remember one boy asked me a question a few weeks into the school year. He said that he had heard that I made learning fun and he could hardly wait to be in my class. I felt so proud until he dropped the bomb and asked, "So what I want to know is, when does the fun start? All we do is work!" Shot down again.

Each year I had a choice to make. I would remind myself that even though September was hard, I believed that the class would come together and something better was ahead. I would daily ask God for wisdom on how best to deal with challenging students and would wait on Him to show me how to reach them. He always did. I would ask the Lord to bless each student and the class as a whole, and over time a calm would settle over the class. Each year I had to ask myself if I was going to focus on the challenge and give up or going to rely on God to give me the wisdom to the sort things out. What God taught me was that the problems were His. God was not surprised by the problems I would encounter, but rather He gave me the patience and wisdom to carry on. The students would settle in and get excited about learning, and the year would quickly roll on.

I hope that you see what I am trying to show you. Cancer or whatever you are facing is going to be a difficult season in your life. You will face new challenges and circumstances, but you will get beyond it if you do not give up. September rolls into October, and many teachers will tell you that the year keeps getting better. It does not happen overnight, and it takes work on everyone's part. We choose to keep going each and every day.

Life brings many changes and challenges that we are not prepared for and others we do not want. We long for the life before change or brokenness entered. We can choose to not deal with our circumstances, loss, or disease and stay in our brokenness. A lovely lady shared how she was totally devastated when her first child was born with seizures and many other challenges. She was not prepared to deal with a child who was not what she was expecting. She felt incapable of going on and was overwhelmed with doubts, fears, and with the "why mes" circling in her mind. She finally sought the help of a counselor who asked her, "Do you still want to be broken and in despair when you are forty or fifty? If you want to get on with life, then you must accept that your life is going to be different from your initial dreams? You have to choose to get on with life that is different from your initial expectations but start to live again." This strong lady fought on and is a proud mother of a delightful young child. Her whole attitude reflects joy and thankfulness for the child God gave her.

Brokenness, trials, or cancer are not the destination. Your struggles are not your whole life and should never define who you are as a person. You are so much more than your problems. Pain, loss, and difficulties will challenge you and change your life for a season or maybe permanently. That is not a truth we want to hear or accept, but God promises that there is more ahead. Your hard times will probably change you and make you question some of your beliefs about yourself and maybe God, but never forget that you are not defined by your circumstances. You are so much more. You can choose to wallow in your misery or look at the current obstacle as a stop along the way to learning something new. It is an adjusting station as you learn to deal with adversity. Each day you have to step out and ask God how to adjust and learn from the day you are given. You will eventually get through this time, changed, but with a future. Are you going to open up your heart to learn what God wants to show you? Are you willing to be changed? Will you allow God to heal your heart? Most of us can use a few rough edges worn off, or at least I can. As you are going through this time, ask the Lord what you can learn from this situation. Take something positive with you. Open your eyes to the positive, and see what God can do when we allow Him. We are held by the mighty right hand of God and loved with an everlasting love. You are safe, sheltered, and cared for each and every second of the day by a God who wants to walk this journey with you.

Your cancer or challenge will change your life, but do not make it your destination. You cannot live your life centered around or obsessed with cancer or any other trial. We all need breaks from our struggles to be refreshed. You also need time away from the treatments and regiments to recharge your battery and enjoy the life you have been given. It can be easy to let the cancer, the procedures, and the treatments become everything. It can be overwhelming, but you need breaks to refocus and just be you. You need time to talk to others and realize they also have problems they are facing. Your situation is not unique. You will struggle at times, but there is a beautiful life out there waiting to be lived. Seize the love, laughter, and joy that God pours down around you each day. Every day look for things to be thankful for. Stop and smell the roses. Start the day with thanksgiving for a new day. Psalm 118:24 (KJV) says, "This is the day the Lord has made; We will rejoice and be glad in." Find what brings you joy, and do it. Don't put off the joy. Don't put off the living because of fear. Live like you have never lived before because you begin to realize that life is short and it is to be cherished and enjoyed. Realize that each day is a gift God has given us. Let these pit stops along the road renew you and fill your tank back up. I have found that time with family and friends laughing, talking, or playing cards made me happy. I have made quilts, gone for walks, led a ladies' Bible study, read books, tried new recipes and gardened. Lastly I even got where I appreciated being able to keep my house neat and tidy. First and foremost, I spent time in prayer or in the word of God. I didn't have time to stop for long.

I have met people who have never gone beyond "the event,"

whether it be cancer, depression, loss of a loved one, or some other hurt. The issue still controls their lives years later. They relive everything each and every day as if they are afraid to let it go. It is like "the event" not only controls their lives but defines who they are. They never reach the next destination because they are frozen in time. I want to share the heartbreaking story of Tamar from 2 Samuel 13.

Tamar was the daughter of King David, and her story is told in 2 Samuel 13. Tamar, described as a beautiful young woman, was raped by her half-brother Amnon when he became obsessed with her. She was devastated by the rape, and then the situation was ignored or mishandled, which led to her giving up all hope. Her father, the king, was furious but did nothing. Her brother Absalom's advice was, "Be quiet for now, my sister; he is your brother. Don't take this thing to heart." How could Tamar not take the rape to heart, she was assaulted. The end results were tragic. King David lost the relationship he had with some of his children. Absalom murdered his brother Amnon, which later led to him trying to overthrow his father as king and his own death.

Tamar had no life. She was the daughter of the king, yet she lived her life in a cage. The next verse says, "And Tamar lived in her brother Absalom's house, a desolate woman." This verse makes me cry when I think of this beautiful woman's life summed up in one word: *desolate*. How could her family forget that she was a daughter of the king? Tamar was hidden and left to deal with despair, hopelessness, depression. Despair leads to low self-esteem and feelings of being unworthy or not good enough and eventually bitterness. This beautiful young woman lost her hope and gave up. She had put her hope in people that left her broken. Proverbs 13:12a (NIV) says, "Hope deferred makes the heart sick." When we lose hope in an area of our life, we slide into deceit. We start believing lies about ourselves or our circumstances. We stay right where we are and convince ourselves we can't or don't deserve to move forward to have a life with purpose or joy again. We park ourselves in despair, sometimes for a lifetime.

Tamar had little control over what happened to her but she lived in desolation. This is never what God wants for anyone. Jeremiah 29:11 (NIV) promises, "'For I know the plans I have for you,' declares the LORD, 'plans to prosper you and not to harm you, plans to give you hope and a future.'" God promises to give hope to those who deeply desire Him. He has good plans for us in His timing. The future will probably be different than you planned, but it will be for good. There is always hope when we call out to the Lord and step out of our self-imposed prisons. Our Savior comes with hope and forgiveness, not recrimination. God's promise in Proverbs 23:18 (NIV) says, "There is surely a future hope for you, and your hope will not be cut off." If God gives a promise, He is true to His promise.

I don't know what to say except don't live your live in fear, shame, pain, or desolation, believing that your life is worth nothing. Don't listen to well-meaning people or lies that circle in your head that make you feel you must live desolate in self-imposed prisons. Choose to call out to God and step out in faith as He leads you back to wholeness. Believe His promises as the second part of Proverbs 13:12 says, "Hope deferred makes the heart sick, but a longing fulfilled is a tree of life." We can never mess up our lives if we call out to God as He shows us how to transform our lives into "trees of life." Hope moves us into action. You can choose to stay where you are, wounded, hurt, disillusioned, and out of control, or you can choose to listen to the prompting of God as He guides your tiny steps back to faith. Choose hope!

We can contrast the story of Tamar with the following story of Peter. This story is in Matthew 14. Peter and the disciples were rowing across a lake, but the wind and waves were keeping them from making any headway. They could do nothing because of the storm. Evening was coming when they noticed that someone was coming toward them walking on the water. At first they thought it was a ghost. Matthew 14:27 (NIV) says, "But Jesus immediately said the them: Take courage! It is I. Don't be afraid." Peter immediately called Jesus and asked to walk out to the Lord on the water. Peter stepped out of the boat and walked out to Jesus on the water. Amazing! Peter took his eyes of Jesus for a bit, started to look around at the storm that was raging, and immediately started to sink. He again called out to Jesus, who took Peter's hand, pulled him out of the water, and they walked back to the boat together. We often focus on the fact that Peter looked at the storm and sank. We forget the fact that Peter actually got out of the boat and walked on the water twice.

Peter could have stayed in the storm tossed boat like the other disciples who huddled in fear, but he didn't. He had to courage to call out to Jesus not once but twice. He called out when he stepped out of the boat and again when he started to sink. Jesus listened and helped him both times and then Jesus calmed the storm. Peter could have chosen to stay in the boat and continue to be thrown around in the storm but he chose something better. He walked on the water with Jesus. He got beyond his fear. Peter took the first baby step and Jesus met him and did the rest.

You may say that your heart is so wounded and shattered that you can't leave the desolation behind. The boat you are in feels safer than stepping out. Take your eyes off the storm, and call out to Jesus. He will hear your prayer and will answer. Jesus will keep coming to help you no matter how many times you sink. Jesus is not counting how many times you fall. He is holding your hand and wanting to teach you how to walk again outside of the storm-tossed boat. I think we all feel like that at times. We feel safer with what we know, even if it is bad, but unfortunately, holding the brokenness close inside will never leave room for the light of God to shine in so you can be healed. We need to release the shattered hopes, hurts, and dreams to God, who alone can heal a broken heart. Healing won't be fast process or without some pain, but in time you will start to feel whole again. Elisabeth Elliot put it this way: "The secret is Christ in me, not me in a different set of circumstances."

The next step on your journey to wholeness is offering pieces of your broken heart to God to be used to encourage others on their journeys to hope. You reach out with a heart of caring and encouragement rather than looking for someone listen to your problems. You offer to share pieces of your shattered life that God is helping make right again to encourage a wounded friend by actively listening and encouraging them to take baby steps toward God. The Holy Spirit will help to show you what to share. James 1:5 (NIV) says, "If any of you lacks wisdom, you should ask God, who gives generously to all without finding fault, and it will be given to you." Friends are reaching out, listening, and encouraging to make room for the hurts to flow away. You can be whole again, somewhat changed, still remembering, but comforted by Jesus so you can in turn comfort others. The Bible explains this process in the following verses from 2 Corinthians 1:3–5 (NIV):

> Praise be to the God and Father of our Lord Jesus
> Christ, the Father of compassion and the God of
> all comfort, who comforts us in all our troubles, so
> that we can comfort those in any trouble with the
> comfort we ourselves receive from God. For just as
> we share abundantly in the sufferings of Christ, so
> also our comfort abounds through Christ.

Start your journey back to God and wholeness. Take the first baby steps. Call out to Jesus, and step out of the boat. Jesus is waiting for you as your life was never meant to be lived in desolation or in a storm-tossed boat. Just reach out your hand and ask for help to get on with your journey. Expect God to hear you cry and to help you. Let your heart be filled with gratitude for all that God plans for you. Jesus is waiting for you. Be encouraged with Isaiah 40:28–31 (NIV):

> Do you not know? Have you not heard? The LORD
> is the everlasting God, the Creator of the ends of
> the earth. He will not grow tired or weary, and

his understanding no one can fathom. He gives
strength to the weary and increases the power of
the weak. Even youths grow tired and weary, and
young men stumble and fall; but those who hope in
the LORD will renew their strength. They will soar
on wings like eagles; they will run and not grow
weary, they will walk and not be faint.

Restore us, O Lord God Almighty; make your
face shine upon us, that we may be saved.
—Psalm 80:19 (NIV)

Whoever dwells in the shelter of the Most High
will rest in the shadow of the Almighty.
I will say of the Lord, "He is my refuge and my fortress,
my God, in whom I trust.
— Psalm 91:1–2 (NIV)

Let us hold unswervingly to the hope we
profess, for he who promised is faithful.
— Hebrews 10:23 (NIV)

CHAPTER 14

Giants and Journeys

*Dream big ... don't let anybody or anything break
your wishbone. Stay strong, full of faith, and
courageous ... keep that backbone straight. And along
the way, don't forget to laugh and enjoy the journey.*

—CHARLES SWINDOLL

I once attended a professional day for teachers that opened with
a keynote speaker before various workshops. The man was
an interesting speaker and had a charismatic way of weaving
stories that made a person want to listen. He spoke of life being a
progression of journeys that we travel. Each journey is different, but
each journey we take contributes to the person we will eventually
become. The outcome of all our journeys is determined by our
attitude. We each choose how we react to what we will learn and
who we meet on the journeys. We can choose to be either positive
or negative. The man had returned from walking across the Sahara
Desert with a group of people. He wove a fascinating story of the
desert and all he learned. The speaker said he was returning home
to a new life journey as his wife and kids had left him. He was
waiting to see what his new journey would bring to his life. It was
very sad. The speaker ended by asking everyone to think about
what are we learning from the journey we were presently taking

and how the people we meet along the way will remember us after we are gone.

I remember thinking about his questions for a long time. How will people I journey with remember me? What effect will my life and its journeys have on others? This was not a question of wins or losses or how many people like me or not. Questions such as: How much baggage am I still carrying from several journeys ago? Is each journey just a repeat of the same issues and reactions in a different setting, or am I learning? Am I reacting positively or negatively? What do people I interact with see in me to remember? Are they seeing Jesus in me?

The last question makes me think of a cute story someone once told me. A young boy left a church service in tears. The pastor had been speaking about the need to ask Jesus into our hearts during his sermon. After church, the pastor found the boy and asked him why he was so upset. The boy replied that he so desired for Jesus to come and live in his heart, but as he was so little and Jesus was a full-grown man, Jesus wouldn't fit. If Jesus lived in him, then Jesus would be sticking out all over. The preacher smiled and told the boy that he was right. When we ask Jesus to live in and through us then His presence should be sticking out all over for the world to see.

Ian, our former pastor, gave a series of sermons of the life of King David maybe ten years ago. I still remember one sermon that was along the same lines as the story I just talked about. The books of 1 and 2 Chronicles tell of the life and reign of King David. He summed up David's life with three points and challenged people to ponder what would be said about us. The first was that David met his giants in life and faced them. He did not back down, run for cover, or cower in fear. Instead David relied on the strength of God to defeat the giants. His giants were everything from fighting Goliath, being a good king, and family problems, to personal issues like when he murdered Uriah. He would admit when he had done wrong and would run to God for forgiveness. He faced the giants by relying on the strength and wisdom of God.

First Samuel 17 tells the story of David defeating the giant, Goliath, who defied the God of Israel. In verses 45–47 (NIV), David said to the Philistine, "You come against me with sword and spear and javelin, but I come against you in the name of the LORD Almighty, the God of the armies of Israel, whom you have defied. This day the LORD will deliver you into my hands, and I'll strike you down and cut off your head … All those gathered here will know that it is not by sword or spear that the LORD saves; for the battle is the LORD's, and he will give all of you into our hands." A little grisly, but that was war back then. My prayer is that I face my giants and stand toe to toe with them. My prayer is that others will also see that they can meet their own giants, not in fear but in the strength of the Lord.

Second, David inspired others to face their giants. Second Samuel 23 tells of the thirty mighty men who followed in David's footsteps to defend the people of Israel. I think we all would love to think that our lives have had a positive influence on those we rub shoulders with. I used to pray and ask God to help me to build up the students I encountered to feel more confident in who they were, in their abilities and self-worth. This is the continual prayer of parents for their children. We all want to be encouragers. The way David lived his life made others want to be better, to become giant slayers like him. As you face your worst fears, others will be watching you. Will others see that I was a giant slayer with the strength of God?

Last, King David stayed true to God. The Bible says that David was a man after God's own heart. We read the story of David, and we can see his strengths but also his glaringly obvious flops. He was a person just like us, but his one desire was to love and please God. Only God knows the secrets of our hearts. First Samuel 16:7 (NIV) says, "The LORD does not look at the things people look at. People look at the outward appearance, but the LORD looks at the heart."

None of us are good enough in ourselves to please a perfectly holy God. That is why Jesus came. He took all our sin upon Himself when He went to the cross to die for each and every person. Romans

6:23 (NIV) says, "For the wages of sin is death, but the gift of God is eternal life in Christ Jesus our Lord." Grace is the love of Jesus that covers all our yuck when we just ask. Ephesians 3:20 (NIV) says, "Now to him who is able to do immeasurably more than all we ask or imagine, according to his power that is at work within us." Philippians 4:19 (NIV) adds, "And my God will meet all your needs according to the riches of his glory in Christ Jesus." Being a child of God is not being perfect. It is trusting in what Jesus accomplished on the cross to make us holy in God's eyes. Grace is God's gift to everyone. It is offered to all but yours to choose or reject. Remember that grace and forgiveness are gifts and never something we earn. We are loved and accepted right where we are and just as we are.

I continue to fight my own giants with the grace of God. Cancer is only one giant among a multitude of giants that we might meet in our lives. We will each face our own giants. Each person's will be different. I will fight my own giants with the strength and grace of God to overcome. God gives me the grace to face my giants but not to fight yours. You must face your own giants in your little corner of the world. Our Lord wants to face them with you, if you but ask.

I wrote the following, "Child of God," several years ago when I was taking a course on who we are in Christ. I asked God to show me what He showered on me each day as a father would to his child. This is what He showed me. Each line is related to a promise from the Bible. It is an example of the love and care that God showers over us even when we are unaware.

Child of God

I am a child of God, and because of this I
have a privileged life of a King's kid.
I am a joint heir with Christ (Romans 8:17).
I'm set apart from the world (1 Peter 2:9).

I'm an alien (foreigner) on a journey as heaven
with God is my home (1 Peter 2:11–12).
God chose me before the beginnings of the world (Ephesians 1:4).
He has given me the mark of Christ that I am His (Galatians 1:6).
God loves me with an everlasting love (Jeremiah 31:3).
My sin has been forgiven as far as the east
is from the west (Psalm 103:12).
God repeatedly forgives my sin and never
gives up on me (1 John 2:1–2).
I've been given a comforter, the Holy Spirit,
who lives in me (1 Corinthians 12).
I have the living word of God so I can know
the heart of God (2 Timothy 3:16).
I have the right to present my prayers, requests, and
thanksgiving before the throne of God (Hebrews 4:16).
Jesus is interceding for me when I do not
know what to pray (Romans 8:26).
Angel are sent by God to guard over me (Psalm 91:11).
God doesn't give up on me (Psalm 139).
A home is being prepared for me in heaven (John 14:1–4).
All the promises in God's Word are mine
to claim (Romans 4:13–25).
God has made plans for me to prosper, to give
me a hope and a future (Jeremiah 29:11).
God has promised to never leave nor forsake me (Hebrews 13:5).
I'm planted by a river that will never run
dry (Jeremiah 17:8, Psalm 1:3).
When the fire and floods come, they will
not destroy me (Isaiah 43:2–4).
I can never be snatch from the mighty
hand of God (John 10:28–29).
I'm kept safe in the shelter of His wings (Psalm 91:4).
I'm the apple of His eye (Psalm 17:8).

I have the promises of the gifts of the Holy
Spirit (1 Corinthians 12:1–11).
I have freedom in Christ when I became a
new creature in Him (Galatians 5:1).
I have a Savior that is a companion who
laughs, cries, speaks, and guides me.
I have Jesus (John 3:36)!
Privileges and rights come with responsibilities.
Love the Lord my God with all my heart, soul, and mind and to
love my neighbor as yourself (Matthew 22:37, Mark 12:30–31).
Honor my Father in heaven (Colossians 3:17,23).
Give thanks in all things (1 Thessalonians 5:18).

Jesus offers every person the privilege of becoming part of the
family of God. Let Jesus fight your giants in His mighty power and
strength. I end with a message and encouragement from the apostle
Paul found in Hebrew.

> Therefore, since we are surrounded by such a great
> cloud of witnesses, let us throw off everything
> that hinders and the sin that so easily entangles.
> And let us run with perseverance the race marked
> out for us, fixing our eyes on Jesus, the pioneer
> and perfecter of faith. For the joy set before him
> he endured the cross, scorning its shame, and
> sat down at the right hand of the throne of God.
> Consider him who endured such opposition from
> sinners, so that you will not grow weary and lose
> heart. (Hebrews 12:1–3 NIV)

CHAPTER 15

Looking to the Future

*Deep, contended joy comes from a place of complete security
and confidence [in God] - even in the midst of trial.*
—CHARLES R. SWINDOLL

Last fall my cancer returned yet again for the third time. It had spread to my brain. I found out that my head was full of cancerous tumors. For a few months, I had noticed that I would get dizzy or lose my sense of balance when I went for walks but did not realize what was going on. My back and spine were becoming painful. Then what I initially thought was flu got worse and worse till I couldn't keep anything down. I had gone to the hospital sick, dizzy, and in pain. God sent a wonderful doctor in emergency who quickly diagnosed the problem and started me on steroids to bring the swelling down in my head and spinal cord. I started radiation treatments for my whole brain a few days later.

The beauty of God's timing is amazing. The month before, at my regular heart checkup, the doctors had found that my heart functions were down for the first time since I had returned to using the drug Herceptin over three years before. God had promised to paint my heart to protect it, and He did as He promised for over three years. The doctors took me off Herceptin to decide what to do and to give my heart a break. Later that same month was when the tumors were found in my head. Therefore, I no longer

121

needed Herceptin. God in his mercy had worked a miracle so my heart could take the drug for as long as I needed it. His timing was perfect. The drug I take now is a relative of the same drug, but this time the chemo also crosses the blood barrier into my brain, where it is needed.

I was sitting with my husband in emergency waiting for the results of the CT scan. I was way on the far side of the noisy emergency room when I heard the phone ring and saw the ER doctor pick up the phone. Somehow I knew it was my results that he was getting. The neat part was that I could hear almost every word that doctor spoke into the phone. I looked at my husband and asked him if he could also hear the conversation. My husband thought I was going crazy as we were sitting in the middle of a noisy room full of people, but I kept telling him what the doctor was saying on the phone. God gave me that small miracle of hearing a quiet conversation across a busy, noisy room to reassure me that He was there with us. We were not alone. The verse from John 14:27 (NIV) was on a reel in my mind. "Peace I leave with you; my peace I give you. I do not give to you as the world gives. Do not let your hearts be troubled and do not be afraid." The emergency doctor asked if my loved ones were near and told us to call them. He gave me steroids to take the swelling down in my brain and spine but did not give me long to live. He said maybe a week, maybe a month if I made it through the night.

The peace I have had from the very beginning was phenomenal. My thoughts and heart were filled with songs of praise and worship from the moment they said, "Cancer has spread to your head, and you have tumors throughout your brain." The songs did not come from me but surrounded me and left me feeling cocooned, safe, and loved. Feelings of uncertainty would come, but the songs would flood my thoughts again. I felt like I was being held in His loving arms. I made it through the night. The funny part was that not only was I allergic to the pain drugs so could not stop scratching, but they also make me so high that I could not stop talking. I was like the Energizer Bunny on steroids. The poor nurses were so patient! Thankfully, the drugs eventually wore off.

The radiation oncologist decided to radiate my whole head because of the number of tumors. The coolest part of all was getting fitted for a radiation mask. I am a bit of a geek about how things work, so I loved the mask. Did you ever watch the movie *The Man in the Iron Mask*? I felt like I could be in the movie except my mask was some kind of malleable plastic. The technicians wet the plastic mask and put it on your face. The plastic, which has many slits to breathe, shrinks super tight to your face as it dries. When you get radiation, they bolt the mask down to the table so the patient is totally still. I find things like this so fascinating. I completed the two weeks of radiation and was given some time to gain strength before starting on new chemo drugs.

Years before I had asked God to give the oncologists wisdom when choosing the drugs they would give me for chemo. I had asked God to give me the strength to endure the drugs given me. I had committed the multitude of drugs into God's hands and asked Him to show me clearly if I was not to carry on with a drug. I have been constantly on a variety of cancer drugs for over twelve years and had faithfully taken everything given to me. After radiation, I was given two new drugs to try. I had to quit one drug for the first time after a few months as it caused too many side effects. I continue on the other chemo drug daily. It is now a year later, and I still have stomach issues from the drugs I take, but I am alive. Praise God.

I needed to use a wheelchair in the hospital as my sense of balance was off. I left using a walker as I was still unsteady on my feet. I switched to a cane over the next month, and now I can go for walks by myself without holding onto anything! What a delight. I am even allowed to drive again. My dear husband was so patient but is glad he no longer has to be relegated to wife walker and taxi service. Each day I would ask God to give me the strength needed to deal with the pain and to get stronger again and to help me lay my concern and worries at His feet.

Our cancer doctor advised my husband and me to deal with the end-of-life tasks and procedures and then to get on with living. The next few weeks my husband and I were busy with dealing with everything from deciding if I wanted to be resuscitated or not, registering for in-home care and hospice care, getting a wheelchair and walker, and talking about personal decision and funeral services with our children. Some discussions were hard, but everyone felt relieved to be able to speak openly and to know everything was in place. I shed more than a few tears but felt surprisingly lighter when everything was done. I was free to focus on getting stronger and living each and every day left to its fullest.

Psalm 139:16 (NIV) says, "Your eyes saw my unformed body; all the days ordained for me were written in your book before one of them came to be." I truly believe that I will live all the days God has given me in spite of the cancer as Christ is control of everything. I have come to realize it is not the number of days I live but how I live those days. Each day is a precious gift. That is one of the blessings of cancer or any terminal disease. People facing the end look at life differently. I know my time may be limited, so I choose how to spend my time wisely. I have come to appreciate friends and people more and do not take them for granted. Time spent with family and friends is precious. I love the small, everyday joys of walks with friends, hugs, warm sunshine, my garden, time with grandkids, laughter, or cooking a meal with my daughters to share. It is like looking at the world after a summer rain when the air is so fresh and clean, filled with vibrant colors. I greet each morning with a smile and a whispered thanks to God that He has chosen to give me another day to be with my loved ones and to know Him better. "This is the day the LORD has made; We will rejoice and be glad in it" (Psalm 118:24 NKJV).

I do not know what the future holds as I try to complete this book. I was advised by the radiation oncologist that all people lose their short-term memory within a year of having radiation to the brain as I did. At this point, I occasionally get muddled with words but have kept my memory, though my loved ones say they notice some differences. We will see what the future brings as I work to finish this book. I do not want to forget God's miracles and faithfulness. I want my daughters and grandchildren to be reminded of God's unfailing love in all circumstances so they remember to, "Be strong and courageous for the Lord is with you wherever you go" (Joshua 1:9). I want them not to just have faith but know deep in their beings that God is always enough for whatever life brings so they never back down from their giants. I want them and you, the reader, to know God is greater than your biggest fears. He is always enough and way more than we could ask, dream of, or ever imagine. Praise His name.

Two weeks ago I met with a new oncologist to go over my yearly tests to see "the big picture." One year since the cancer went to my brain! I had over the weeks before had several tests and scans and was driving down to hear the results. I was praying, and I could hear God whisper in my heart, "Be still and know that I am God. My grace is sufficient for all your needs." Now this is what God has whispered each time I have had bad news. I asked God to help me face the news. He whispered again, "Why do you worry? Maybe I just want to awe you." The oncologist asked if I had any questions. I told her that I first needed to hear the test results and then I would ask more mundane questions. Her answer was, "Awesome, you are doing awesome for now." I could see the smile on Jesus's face as tears slowly ran down my face in thanksgiving.

What days I have left will be spent rejoicing in the Lord as He is mighty to save. Cancer has entered my life and tried to knock me down and destroy me. It has dealt some powerful blows, but every time God has met those blows with His grace and strength. A couple from our church gave me a card that said something like, "Remember cancer is always the 'little c' when you belong to Christ, who is always the 'Big C.'" Big C always wins over little c. What a great perspective to remember.

The enemy has used cancer to try to destroy my faith and take my hope. No way! Satan tried to use little c to tell me that cancer was my fault and I was not good enough for God. Big C continues to tell me, "I have loved you with an everlasting love; I have drawn you with unfailing kindness" (Jeremiah 31:3 NIV).

Little c will tell you to hold your fears in your tightly fisted hand. Big C tells us to open our hands up and let His love and light fill our hearts with His love. Big C offers to carry all our burdens and pain and continually picks you up when you fall down.

Little c tells you that giving control of the situation to God makes you weak. Big C wants to come along beside you to help you and restore your hope. Psalm 34:17–19 (NIV) says,

> The righteous cry out, and the Lord hears them; he delivers them from all their troubles. The Lord is close to the brokenhearted and saves those who are crushed in spirit. The righteous person may have many troubles, but the Lord delivers him from them all.

Little c tells me I am useless as I get words muddled and I am not able to do what I used to do. Big C says in 2 Corinthians 12:9 (NIV), "But he said to me, 'My grace is sufficient for you, for my power is made perfect in weakness.' Therefore I will boast all the more gladly about my weaknesses, so that Christ's power may rest on me." I am physically weaker, but my spirit is filled with the power of the Holy Spirit. I am a loved and valued person in the eyes of God and my loved ones.

Little c says that all my trials are because I am worthless or somehow less. Big C says In Job 23:10 (NIV), "But he knows the way that I take; when he has tested me, I will come forth as gold." Billy Graham in *Hope for Each Day*, puts it this way:

> Affliction can be a means of refining and of purification. Just as ore must pass through the

refiner's furnace before it can yield up its gold, so our lives must sometimes pass through God's furnace of affliction before they can bring forth something beautiful and useful to Him ... Affliction can also make us stronger in our faith and develop our confidence in God's watch care over us. It may also drive us back to the right path when we have wandered. David said, *"Before I was afflicted I went astray, but now I obey your word" (Psalm 119:67 NIV).* Whatever the reason, if God sends affliction your way, take it in faith as a blessing, not a curse.

The enemy tried to use little c to destroy my self-confidence by taking my ability to continue with my job of teaching but Big C has shown me I am much more than just a job. I am a much-loved child of the king. My worth and value is seated with Him. He had a purpose in creating me, and He still has a purpose for me.

Little c took my hair, but big C gives me beauty. The beauty of Jesus shining through and around me. He also gave me beautiful curls each time it my hair has returned.

Little c has taken much of my physical strength. Big C gives strength and wisdom to not only meet the needs of each day but to bear fruit.

But blessed is the one who trusts in the LORD, whose confidence is in him. They will be like a tree planted by the water that sends out its roots by the stream. It does not fear when heat comes; its leaves are always green. It has no worries in a year of drought. (Jeremiah 17:7–8)

Little c tries to destroy my cells and heart and even my life, but it can never, ever have me. I belong to Big C. I was purchased with the blood Jesus shed so I could become His beloved child. Big C reminds me that my name is tattooed on His hand. He knows my name. He knows the number of hairs on my head, which at times are not many! I belong to God, and nothing can remove me from His care.

> How precious to me are your thoughts, God!
> How vast is the sum of them!
> Were I to count them,
> they would outnumber the grains of sand—
> when I awake, I am still with you.
> —Psalm 139:17–18 (NIV)

Little c tells me I have no hope. Big C tells me that my hope is in Him and nothing can be taken from me. Proverbs 23:18 (NIV) says, "There is surely a future hope for you, and your hope will not be cut off."

Little c tries to tell me that my problems are too big for Big C and I'm all by myself. Big C promises us that if He is for us, who can be against us? Romans 8:37–39 (NIV) promises, "No, in all these things we are more than conquerors through him who loved us. For I am convinced that neither death nor life, neither angels nor demons, neither the present nor the future, nor any powers, neither height nor depth, nor anything else in all creation, will be able to separate us from the love of God that is in Christ Jesus our Lord."

Little c says cancer is determines my life and death only. Big C says that my time is held in His hands, and when my time is completed, then and only then will I leave this earth to join with Jesus forever. John 3:16–17 (NIV) says, "For God so loved the world that he gave his one and only Son, that whoever believes in him shall not perish but have eternal life. For God did not send his Son into the world to condemn the world, but to save the world through him."

Little c continues to try to steal my life and my future. Big C promises that when we place our trust in Jesus, life is only beginning. Jesus tells us in John 14:1–3 (NIV):

Do not let your hearts be troubled. You believe in God; believe also in me. My Father's house has many rooms; if that were not so, would I have told you that I am going there to prepare a place for you? And if I go and prepare a place for you, I will come back and take you to be with me that you also may be where I am.

Little c encourage us to hide by ourselves in fear and apathy. Big C remembers us to open up our fears to Jesus who wants to heal hearts. Jesus fills our hearts again to joy and peace until our hearts are overflowing as we worship and praise Jesus.

> I will extol the LORD at all times;
> his praise will always be on my lips.
> I will glory in the LORD;
> let the afflicted hear and rejoice.
> Glorify the LORD with me;
> let us exalt his name together.
> I sought the LORD, and he answered me;
> he delivered me from all my fears.
> Those who look to him are radiant;
> their faces are never covered with shame.
> —Psalm 34:1–5 (NIV)

Remember, your greatest fear can only destroy what you allow it to have. Lay your greatest fears and struggles down at the feet of Jesus. He wants to walk with you and carry your burdens. Choose hope, choose the Big C, and live for Christ. Choose to dance in the rain and to find the biggest puddle to just splash in. Choose to look up and see all the stars when it is the darkest. Choose to see the blessings and not only the trials. The blessings are all around you if you just look for them. Jesus is showering them down on you if you but look for them. Remember to say thank you!

Last, little c can never take away my greatest hope, which is held in trust me by Jesus. Big C in said it best in Job 19:25–27 (NIV), "I know that my redeemer lives, and that in the end he will stand on the earth. And after my skin has been destroyed, yet in my flesh I will see God; I myself will see him with my own eyes—I, and not another. How my heart yearns within me!" Our destiny is held in trust in the hand of our Lord, and no one can steal that away. I will not be meeting a stranger but a friend who has walked beside me and allowed me to know Him.

I often spend time with Jesus in the meadow on the mountaintop that God showed me in the vision I shared earlier. We walk along the river, and I love the spray of the beautiful waterfalls. I feel refreshed and stronger after spending time with Jesus there. Recently while I was in the meadow, Jesus led me to the edge of the valley and pointed down at the valley that stretched out far below me. It was far in the distance, and there was no river or grass growing. The light was a different color. It looked so far away, and I told Jesus I never wanted to go there as I felt so safe with Him in the little meadow. Jesus seemed to open my ears and heart, and I could hear the moaning and agony of the people in the valley. The pain was overwhelming, and it hurt to hear. Jesus pointed to me and then the valley.

I asked Him what He wanted me to do, and the answer was Mark 16:15 (NIV), "Go into all the world and preach the gospel to all creation." I was overwhelmed by His request. How could I go into the world? I can't travel the world with brain cancer. Go where? Do what? I am sick. Jesus whispered that He knew, but that He would go with me to give me the strength to do all that was needed. He whispered, "The people are hurting. Someone needs to tell them that how that I (God) love them and how I desire to heal their hearts and lives. So Liz, go and tell them. Go and tell them how much I love them."

I have little to offer, but I gave Jesus all I had that day. What else could I do when I know how wonderful a life with Christ can be. Jesus went on to reassure me with promises like the following. Philippians 4:13 (NIV) says, "Can do all this through him who gives me strength." Then came the reminder. "So do not fear, for I am with you; do not be dismayed, for I am your God. I will strengthen you and help you; I will uphold you with my righteous right hand" (Isaiah 41:10 NIV). Then the last reassurance was, "Behold, I am with you always, until the end of the age" (Matthew 28:20 NIV). I am reminded of a saying that my mom kept on her fridge for years. It simply said, "One man with God is always the majority."

This was when God started to plant the thoughts in my heart to write this book. Writing does not come easy to me, but I have tried to write what God has put in my heart. I repeat my prayer from the first chapter as I finish: "May God bless the words I have written. May they be an encouragement and challenge to live your life in the hope that only comes from God. Pull out your stones of remembrance regularly, and reflect on the blessings showered on you. Be thankful, and never stop believing that you are constantly loved by an extraordinary God that will never leave or forsake you. Let your heart be awed by His goodness."

There is an old hymn called, "When the Roll Is Called Up Yonder" by James M. Black. The following is the first verse and chorus.

When the trumpet of the Lord shall sound,
and time shall be no more,
And the morning breaks, eternal, bright and fair;
When the saved of earth shall gather over on the other shore,
And the roll is called up yonder, I'll be there.

When the roll is called up yonder,
When the roll is called up yonder,
When the roll is called up yonder,
When the roll is called up yonder, I'll be there.

I know that when my time is over that I will go to be with Jesus as He has promised. I will be at that roll call the song sings about. What a day of rejoicing that will be. My hope and prayer is that all my loved ones and friends will also be there, including you who reads this book. I will not say good-bye but rather, "Meet you at roll call."

Do not let your hearts be troubled. You believe in God; believe also in me. My Father's house has many rooms; if that were not so, would I have told you that I am going there to prepare a place for you? And if I go and prepare a place for you, I will come back and take you to be with me that you also may be where I am. You know the way to the place where I am going. (John 14:1–4 NIV)

"Though the mountains be shaken and the hills be removed, yet my unfailing love for you will not be shaken nor my covenant of peace be removed," says the Lord, who has compassion on you. (Isaiah 54:10 NIV)

The Lord God is a sun and shield; The Lord will give grace and glory; No good thing will He withhold From those who walk uprightly. (Psalm 84:11 NLT)

To him who is able to keep you from stumbling and to present you before his glorious presence without fault and with great joy— to the only God our Savior be glory, majesty, power and authority, through Jesus Christ our Lord, before all ages, now and forevermore! Amen. (Jude 1:24–25 NIV)

BIBLIOGRAPHY

Charles Swindoll, "The Poem Attitude," http://thelittlerebellion.
com/index.php/2012/11/new-club-on-campus-embraces-
bodies-and-beauty/bbp-poem-2/

Charles Swindoll, Quotes by Charles Swindoll, Charles R Swindoll
Quotes, https://www.brainyquote.com/quotes/authors/c/
charles_r_swindoll.html, https://www.goodreads.com/author/
quotes/5139.Charles_R_Swindoll

Max Lucado, *Life Lessons with Max Lucado, Philippians.* Nashville,
TN: Thomas Nelson Inc., 2007, 19.

Nick Vujicic, *Unstoppable, The Incredible Power of Faith in Action.*
Colorado Springs, CO: WaterBrook Press, 2012, 12.

Elisabeth Elliot, *The Quiet Heart.* Grand Rapids, MI: Fleming H. Revell
Company, 2004 (first published 1995). http://www.goodreads.
com/quotes/618800-the-secret-is-christ-in-me-not-me-in-a

Billy Graham, *Hope for Each Day.* Nashville, TN: Thomas Nelson,
2006.

Printed in the United States
By Bookmasters